The Children Who Lived

The Children Who Lived

Using Harry Potter and Other Fictional
Characters to Help Grieving Children
and Adolescents

Kathryn A. Markell and Marc A. Markell

Illustrations by Morgan K. Carr-Markell

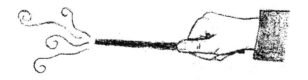

Routledge
Taylor & Francis Group
New York   London

The authors have received permission from J. K. Rowling to include quotes from her books in this work. The themes and interpretations arguments in this book however, are not necessarily shared by J. K. Rowling and this book is not endorsed by her. All writing exercises included in this book are intended for personal use only.

Routledge
Taylor & Francis Group
270 Madison Avenue
New York, NY 10016

Routledge
Taylor & Francis Group
2 Park Square
Milton Park, Abingdon
Oxon OX14 4RN

© 2008 by Taylor & Francis Group, LLC
Routledge is an imprint of Taylor & Francis Group, an Informa business

Printed in the United States of America on acid-free paper
10 9 8 7 6 5 4 3 2 1

International Standard Book Number-13: 978-0-415-95765-6 (Softcover)

Library of Congress Cataloging-in-Publication Data

Markell, Kathryn A.
    The children who lived : using Harry Potter and other fictional characters to help grieving children and adolescents / by Kathryn A. Markell and Marc A. Markell ; illustrations by Morgan K. Carr-Markell.
        p. cm.
        Includes bibliographical references (p.) and index.
        ISBN 978-0-415-95765-6 (softcover)
        1. Grief in children. 2. Bereavement in children. 3. Grief in adolescence. 4. Bereavement in adolescence. 5. Characters and characteristics in literature. I. Markell, Marc A. II. Title.

BF723.G75M26 2008
155.9'37083--dc22   2007041132

Visit the Taylor & Francis Web site at
http://www.taylorandfrancis.com

and the Routledge Web site at
http://www.routledge.com

Dedication

We would like to dedicate this book to our dad, Bill Markell, whose life and death are an important part of the story of our lives. Katie would also like to dedicate the book to Jim Carr and Morgan Carr-Markell, the loves of her life. Marc would also like to dedicate the book to Ed Breun and Eli Carr, who he loves with all his heart and who teach him every day what it means to live well and love well.

Contents

SECTION 2: FOUR OTHER NOVELS TO HELP GRIEVING CHILDREN AND ADOLESCENTS

SECTION 3: GAMES

SECTION 4: MORE CRAFT IDEAS

Acknowledgments

We would like to thank Morgan Carr-Markell, an enthusiastic Harry Potter fan, for her illustrations and editing. We would like to thank Haiyun Lu, also a devoted Harry Potter fan, for her feedback on Section 1 of our book. We would also like to thank Ed Breun and Jim Carr for their technical assistance and ongoing support.

Introduction: The Children Who Lived

Grieving children and adolescents are, like Harry Potter in the novels by J.K. Rowling, the boys and girls "who lived." They have experienced the death of someone they care about. Now they need to find a way to deal with their grief, and to continue on without the person they have lost.

Children and adolescents often identify with the fictional characters in the stories they read, and the way that these characters handle their problems may help children to cope with similar issues in their own lives. This book outlines activities to help grieving children and adolescents by focusing on fictional child and adolescent characters experiencing grief in eleven novels.

The majority of the book focuses on activities and discussions based on the characters in the seven Harry Potter novels by J.K. Rowling: *Harry Potter and the Sorcerer's Stone*, *Harry Potter and the Chamber of Secrets*, *Harry Potter and the Prisoner of Azkaban*, *Harry Potter and the Goblet of Fire*, *Harry Potter and the Order of the Phoenix*, *Harry Potter and the Half-Blood Prince*, and *Harry Potter and the Deathly Hallows*. The Harry Potter novels are a rich source for themes and issues related to grief and loss.

However, because certain grief issues are not addressed in the Harry Potter novels, and since some children may relate more to characters from other stories, grieving characters from the following four novels are also included: *Charlotte's Web* by E.B. White, *The Secret Garden* by Frances Hodgson Burnett, *Where the Red Fern Grows* by Wilson Rawls, and *Ordinary People* by Judith Guest.

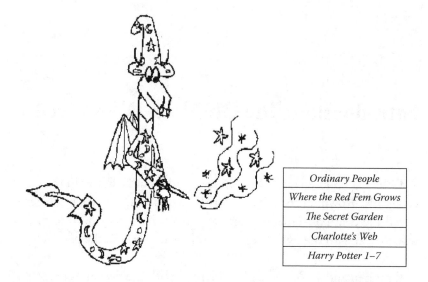

| Ordinary People |
| Where the Red Fern Grows |
| The Secret Garden |
| Charlotte's Web |
| Harry Potter 1–7 |

Harry Potter and the other fictional characters analyzed in this book, like many grieving children and adolescents, find that grieving is a complicated process. They experience not only sadness and longing, but also anger, guilt and regret.

The grieving child's experience of loss makes him or her different from many of their peers, and may even become an important part of the child's developing identity. In a time when life expectancy is increasing, more and more children and adolescents are reaching adulthood without experiencing the death of someone important to them. Those that do may feel not only grief, but also that they have been "singled out." That can be especially difficult at a time in life when it is common to wish you were exactly like everyone else.

In Harry's case, as in the case of many children, the loss of his parents is synonymous with the loss of many other things: the loss of attention, the loss of love, and the loss of caring role models to turn to for advice. For Harry, these losses are experienced again and again, as he compares himself to his spoiled cousin Dudley, who gets ample attention from his parents, and later to his friend Ron, who has grown up in a large and loving family. Luckily Harry finds many people in the wizarding world, both adults and children, who care about him and help him to deal with his grief.

Other grieving fictional children and adolescents do not have the support that Harry finds in his wizarding world. In *The Secret Garden*,

Mary and Colin have been emotionally abandoned by adults to deal with their grief and their development by themselves. In the first half of the book, they have become pessimistic and angry children who no one, child or adult, wants to be around. At age 10, almost the same age as Harry is at the beginning of *Harry Potter and the Sorcerer's Stone*, they find each other, and they find other children, Dickon and Martha, to help them see the world more positively. Just as the magic of the wizarding world helps Harry to heal and grow, the magic of the secret garden helps Mary and Colin to blossom.

In *Ordinary People*, we find that sometimes family and friends are not enough to help children and adolescents cope with the death of someone important to them. After the death of Conrad's brother in a boating accident, Conrad feels overwhelming grief. Conrad misses his brother, and the "normal" family life he had, and he also feels guilty that he survived the boating accident when his brother did not. Conrad's mother is so upset about the death of one of her son's that she cannot help the other. When Conrad attempts suicide to end the pain of his grief, his mother is not there to support him. Conrad finds that seeing a psychiatrist, Dr. Berger, helps him to feel better. He has not been able to talk to any of his family or friends about how he is feeling. Just as Harry Potter feels stressed when his friend Cho wants to talk about the death of their mutual friend Cedric, Conrad feels overwhelmed when the friends of his dead brother want to discuss their grief with Conrad. Dr. Berger helps Conrad to see that he is not at fault for his brother's death, and that sometimes grieving parents cannot help their children to deal with their loss.

For many children, their first experience of grief and loss comes after the death of a pet. The focus of both *Charlotte's Web* and *Where the Red Fern Grows* is on the life and death of animals. Charlotte the spider helps Wilbur the pig, and the readers of *Charlotte's Web*, to understand that death is a part of life. She shows him how important loyal friends are in helping anyone through the rough times in life. Billy, in *Where the Red Fern Grows*, is also a ten-year-old child at the beginning of the story. He has saved money for two years to buy two hound dogs. He is finally able to buy two puppies that he names Old Dan and Little Ann. He hunts with these dogs almost every day, and eventually enters them in a contest. Just as Hagrid's many pets in the Harry Potter books are important to him, Old Dan and Little Ann are as important to Billy as his friends and family members. When their pets and animal friends die, both Hagrid and Billy grieve.

The issues, discussion questions, activities, craft projects and games presented in this book are designed to help grieving children and adolescents (and maybe some adults too) deal with grief and loss issues by identifying with grieving fictional characters and with fictional worlds. The authors hope that the variety of issues and activities presented in this book will help adults working with grieving children and adolescents to find the themes and activities that will work best with that specific child. For example, one grieving child may find that **Theme 1: The Mirror of Erised** activities and discussion are helpful to them, while another may find that focusing on **Theme 2: Harry's Scar**, or **Theme 50: True Names for Pets** about pet loss, is more helpful.

Children and adolescents realize that all stories must come to an end. This realization does not diminish the pleasure of reading good stories, or stop people from rereading them. Reading a story can change the reader's life and rereading it can give them new insights each time. In the "real world," when someone dies, the story of their life and death lives on and continues to affect those who knew them. But after someone dies, people may not know how to talk about that life anymore, and they may be reluctant or afraid to discuss that person's death. Some fictional characters are as real to their readers as friends and family. Reading and rereading the story of a character's loss and how he or she copes with grief, can be a model for grieving readers, and can give readers hope.

The lives of real people, as well as the lives of fictional characters, show us that there is no one "right way" to grieve. Although the lives of characters are often complicated, they are "concrete" and unchanging in ways that are usually not true for living people. Therefore, it may be easier for some children to relate to fictional characters who they identify with, and to apply what the characters are going through to their own lives.

The Authors' Story

We are siblings. Our father died when we were very young (Katie was seven years old and Marc was five years old), in 1963. Our mother was left to raise five children (ranging in age from one to eight years of age) by herself. There was little support available for grieving adults at that time, let alone for grieving children. In the small town we grew up in, we sometimes felt identified as the "children whose dad had died." We knew few other children who had lost a parent to death, and we never talked to anyone, inside or outside of our family, about our grief.

In talking to each other about our father's death later in our lives, we realize that we divided our childhood into two parts: before our "daddy" died and after he died. Before he died, our father was a carpenter, and our mother was a "stay at home mom," caring for five children. Our father often took on extra work in the evenings to make ends meet, and so we did not see him as often as we wished. Some of our fondest memories of our father are of combing his hair while he sat on the couch after Sunday dinner. He always kept a small comb in his pocket, and we would take turns combing his rather greasy Brylcreemed hair into what we believed were fashionable hairstyles. Our mother would sometimes tell us to stop bothering our father, but he was always patient with our hair combing, and told her to let us be.

One morning our father had such bad stomach pains that he had to be rushed to the hospital. Katie was already at school, but Marc remembers wiping his shoes off as he lay on the couch, so that they would be clean in the car going to the hospital. We never saw our father alive again. His stomach had split open, and he spent one week in the hospital as the doctors tried to battle all the complications that ensued. He died on June 4, 1963 at the age of 44. His death certificate said that the cause of death was pneumonia. On that day, seven-year-old Katie came home from school to find five-year-old Marc waiting for her in the yard. He said there was some bad news. She told him she didn't want to hear it. They both went into the house, where their mom and grandmother were sitting with one of the priests from the church. Katie was told what Marc already knew: their father was dead.

For the next several days, everything was disorganized. Neighbors put us to bed at night while our mother tried to sort everything out. On the day that our mother picked out our father's casket, we followed our older brother and one of his friends several miles across town. We were scared and excited to be so far from home, and worried that people would be angry with us for leaving without telling anyone. But when we returned, we realized that things really were different. No one had even noticed that we had been gone.

At the wake, our father looked so different lying in his casket. We both remember that he had a spot on his nose that had not been there before. People kept telling us that the good die young, and that worried us. Someone had bought Katie a new navy dress that had a matching jacket. She loved the dress, and felt very guilty for being glad that she got to wear it. After the funeral mass, Katie remembers the hearse driving by the school playground on the way to the cemetery. She felt strange missing school.

It rained while our father's casket was lowered into the ground, and many of the women there took off their shoes to walk through the wet grass back to the cars, so as not to ruin them. We had a reception at our house after the funeral. People had brought us so much food, including Rice Krispie bars, which we both liked.

That summer our maternal grandmother moved in with us. Our car was always parked in the driveway, because neither our mother nor grandmother knew how to drive. They had never had a close relationship with each other, and now they began to argue often. At the end of the summer, our mother got her license and later in the fall she got a job at the Montgomery Ward's store in town.

When Marc started kindergarten in September, he cried every day, because he worried that our mother would die while he was at school. Although Marc remembers that the teacher yelled at him and told him to stop being a baby, she finally let our mom come to school with Marc, and stay for shorter and shorter periods of time each day until he could let her leave without crying.

Sometimes when we misbehaved, our grandmother would tell us that they might have to put us all in an orphanage if we did not behave better. Katie remembers worrying about how she would keep us all together in the orphanage. She thought going to the orphanage was inevitable, because we could never seem to stop misbehaving.

Although we did not talk about it until we were adults, both of us imagined that our father was living in a cabin in heaven. We thought he was sitting on his porch visiting with other relatives who had died, smoking his pipe, and waiting for us to join him someday. Probably someone had told us that this was what heaven was like.

We tell this story because, like so many other children "who live" through a death of a significant person, the death of our father, even more than 40 years later, remains one of our most vivid memories. It profoundly affected our lives and continues to shape our lives in unexpected ways.

Although no one ever suggested that we see a counselor or talk about our grief, we both did find guidance and consolation in books. Katie remembers reading *Five Little Peppers and How They Grew* by Margaret Sidney over and over. It told the story of a widowed mother with five children. The family was very close, and always looked out for one another. She also read *Little Women* by Louisa May Alcott many times. She identified with Jo. She was sad that Beth died, but also happy that Jo still went on to live a happy life, even without her beloved sister.

Marc was not an avid reader as a child, but the first book he remembers reading all the way through by himself was *Angel Unaware* by the singer Dale Evans Rogers. It told the story of the only child of Dale Evans and Roy Rogers, Robin Elizabeth, who died of complications of Down syndrome at age two.

Perhaps not surprisingly, as we grew older, we both developed an interest in helping children and adolescents, and we both grew up to become psychologists and teachers. Marc was a special education teacher for many years, and then returned to school to get a Ph.D. in Educational Psychology from the University of Minnesota. He now teaches at St. Cloud State University, helping to prepare college students to become special education teachers. He is also a certified thanatologist, and frequently conducts workshops about grief issues. Katie received her Ph.D. in Psychology at Loyola University Chicago, and has taught college level psychology classes, including Child and Adolescent Development and Death and Dying, for more than twenty years. She presently teaches at Anoka-Ramsey Community College.

Like millions of other people, in 1998, we became enthusiastic fans of J. K. Rowling's amazing Harry Potter novels after someone gave Katie's daughter a copy of the first book. In 2002, we joined a wonderful organization called the Association for Death Education and Counseling. These two interests led to the work presented in this book. We realized that we, like Harry and so many real-life children, were part of a special group: the children who lived.

How to Use This Book

Example focusing on: **Theme 1: The Mirror of Erised**

This book is separated into sections. The first section contains themes and activities for grieving children and adolescents related to the seven Harry Potter novels by J.K. Rowling: *Harry Potter and the Sorcerer's Stone, Harry Potter and the Chamber of Secrets, Harry Potter and the Prisoner of Azkaban, Harry Potter and the Goblet of Fire, Harry Potter and the Order of the Phoenix, Harry Potter and the Half-Blood Prince*, and *Harry Potter and the Deathly Hallows*. The second section focuses on themes and activities connected to four other novels: *Charlotte's Web* by E.B. White, *The Secret Garden* by Frances Hodgson Burnett, *Where the Red Fern Grows* by Wilson Rawls and *Ordinary People* by Judith Guest. The third section contains games that can be used to help grieving children and adolescents, and the fourth section presents additional craft ideas, not presented in the book theme activities, that may help grieving children and adolescents.

The issues and activities included in the book encompass a wide range of reactions, problems, and feelings that grieving children and adolescents may experience. Each book theme is designed to work as a "stand alone" discussion and activity unit. Therefore, there is some overlap between the questions and activities described for different themes. Sometimes related themes are noted in the text of a theme's overview by a "see also" note accompanied by the figure of Solace the Story Dragon. There are activities that involve Solace the Story Dragon in Section 3 of the book.

Solace the Story Dragon

Adults using the book to help children or adolescents will want to pick and choose from among themes that they think will help any specific child or adolescent (and maybe a grieving adult too!).

When applicable, chapter numbers from the novel being discussed that relate to the theme are noted. **It may be helpful to have children or adolescents read the parts of the book that are related to the themes before going to the theme discussion questions or activities.** Even people who have read the various novels may not be able to remember all the helpful novel details! **Spoiler warning:** the theme guidelines assume that you have read all of the books! A brief glossary at the end of the book can help readers define unfamiliar terms.

The games and craft activities in Sections 3 and 4 of the book focus mostly on the Harry Potter novels, but they can be easily adapted to other books. The CD in the back of the book contains all the worksheets that are shown "in miniature" in the text of the chapters. These are in both PowerPoint and JPEG formats. In PowerPoint, the reader can more easily choose the ones that they would like to use. It may be helpful, when printing the sheets, to select "landscape" orientation and letter paper size.

Theme 1: The Mirror of Erised (Including Guidelines for Using All the Themes)

When people have experienced the death of someone they care about, it is common for them to wish that they could see that person again. The longing for the dead person may also be a longing for the end to the pain of grief, and a wish for "everything to be back to normal." While there is no "right way" for a child to grieve, some children may spend so much time longing for the person they have lost, and for the past with that person, that they have trouble living their lives in the present and planning for the future.

There are several places in the Harry Potter books where Harry and other characters spend so much time dwelling on their losses, or on what they long to be true, that they have trouble dealing with their life as it is.

Rowling tells us that, like many unhappy children, Harry dreams of unknown relatives coming to take him away to a better life (Book 1, Ch. 2). After learning about his parents from Hagrid, Harry is understandably curious about them, and he is somewhat jealous of his friends, like Ron, who have living, loving parents who they can count on.

When Harry accidentally finds the Mirror of Erised in Book 1, Ch. 12 (Erised is desire spelled backward), he sees his parents in the mirror, along with a large group of other dead relatives, all waving and smiling lovingly at him. He returns to visit the mirror several times until the Headmaster Dumbledore tells Harry that he is moving the mirror, and asks Harry not to go looking for it, because "It does not do to dwell on dreams and forget to live..." (Book 1, Ch. 12, p. 214). In Book 7, Ch. 35, p. 719, Harry finds out that, as a young man, Dumbledore had many losses in his own life. Rowling writes, "At last he (Harry) knew what Dumbledore would have seen when he looked in the Mirror of Erised, and why Dumbledore had been so understanding of the fascination it had exercised over Harry."

The discussion and activities explore why it may be a problem to dwell on loss too much, and how children can acknowledge loss and still live their lives.

Before going to the discussion questions or activities, the children or adolescents could read Book 1, Ch. 12.

Possible Discussion Questions

The discussion questions that accompany all of the themes are meant as a way to help the grieving child or adolescent discuss his or her feelings, and connect his or her experience to that of the fictional character that the theme includes. They can be used alone, or with the theme activities. There are usually many questions presented with each theme. The person using the theme should choose the discussion questions they feel most apply to the child or adolescent they are working with. If a child or adolescent does not seem comfortable responding to discussion questions, he or she may be more comfortable expressing their feelings by doing an activity that accompanies the theme.

- What does the child or adolescent think they would see if they looked into the Mirror of Erised? Why would they see this?
- If the child says they would see the person who died in the mirror, they could be asked if they would keep visiting the mirror if they could?
- If they kept visiting the mirror, what might they miss out on in life?
- What might the person who died see if they looked in this mirror? Explain.
- Is Dumbledore right to ask Harry to stop visiting the mirror? Why or why not?
- How would they feel if they had found the Mirror of Erised, and then it had been taken away?
- What might Harry miss out on at Hogwarts (or in life) if he keeps visiting the mirror?
- If Harry was their friend, and he asked them to help him find the mirror again, what would they tell him?
- After reading Book 7, the child or adolescent could discuss what they think Dumbledore would have seen if he looked in the Mirror of Erised, and why.
- What other activities help Harry to stop dwelling on the mirror?
- What does Hagrid give Harry at the end of the book (Book 1, Ch. 17), before he returns to the Dursleys? Does this help Harry?
- Is it ever difficult for them to stop thinking about the person who died? Does it get in the way of other parts of their life?

- What activities help them to dwell less on the person who died and/or some aspects of their death?
- What is their favorite picture of the person they have lost?

Activities

The activities that accompany each theme can be used alone, or with the discussion questions, to help children and adolescents express and explore their feelings of grief. The person working with the child can choose which of the activities given for each theme may best help the child they are working with. The age and interests of the child may be helpful factors in this choice. Each worksheet appearing in "miniature" in a theme's activity section can also be found on the CD in the back of the book under the noted worksheet number. For example, the first worksheet noted below would be found on the CD under Worksheet 1. In addition to the activities that accompany each theme, adults could also use the games in Section 3 of the book with the child or adolescent they are working with, or the additional craft projects outlined in Section 4.

- Have children draw a picture of (and possibly write about) what they would see in the Mirror of Erised (see worksheet), or have adolescents write what they would see if they looked in the Mirror of Erised.

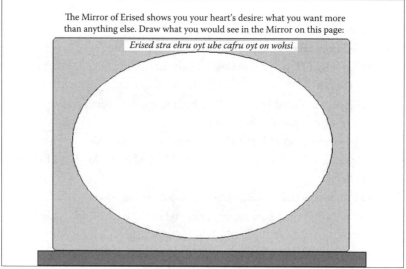

The Mirror of Erised shows you your heart's desire: what you want more than anything else. Draw what you would see in the Mirror on this page:

Erised stra ehru oyt ube cafru oyt on wohsi

- Have the children write or draw what the person who died might have seen in the Mirror of Erised?
- Have the children make a Mirror of Erised from a plastic frame. First they can place a drawing of what they would see when they looked in the mirror into the frame. Then they could consider what their dreams are for their present and future, and place a drawing of that over their previous drawing. In that way, their dreams or wishes are still in the mirror, but they are not visible, because their focus, like Harry's after he stops visiting the mirror, is now on their life in the present and future.
- The child could write a "secret message" backward to themselves or to the person who died. The message would appear "frontward" when held up to a mirror.

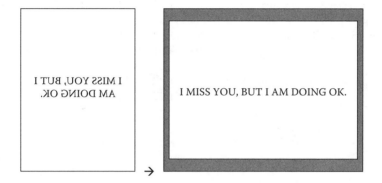

Guide to Using the Themes

Helping Children and Adolescents With:	Theme #'s
Anger/Guilt	16, 20, 37, 38, 48, 51, 52, 54
Fears/Bad Dreams	22, 25, 27, 32, 37, 38
Identity Issues	2, 3, 4, 5, 6, 9, 12, 29, 34, 35, 42, 46, 52, 55, 56
Loneliness	45, 46
Non-Death Losses	7, 23
Pet Loss	19, 50
Promises	28
Remembering and Living Now	1, 3, 4, 8, 9, 15, 16, 18, 21, 24, 30, 31, 33, 35, 36, 42
Sadness/Depression/Negative Thoughts	7, 15, 16, 17, 22, 23, 25, 31, 37, 38, 41, 46, 53
Seeking Support/Healing	8, 10, 12, 14, 15, 17, 24, 25, 26, 27, 29, 31, 32, 34, 36, 39, 40, 43, 44, 47, 49, 52, 53, 54, 55
Talking About/Understanding Death	2, 8, 11, 12, 13, 14, 18, 20, 30, 37, 38, 43, 47, 48, 51, 52, 53, 56

1

Using the Harry Potter Books by J. K. Rowling to Help Grieving Children and Adolescents

Like many of the best children's stories, the Harry Potter books are filled with loss and death. Although these real-life issues are experienced in a magical world, not even wizards can easily explain them or take away their pain. But literature, like magic, can open up new worlds for people. It can show them a myriad of ways to look at problems, and many possible ways to survive losses and challenges, and even flourish beyond them.

Many children who have experienced the death of someone they care about grow up, like Harry Potter, not even knowing that they have the need or the right to grieve. Harry is told by his uncaring and abusive aunt and uncle, the Dursleys, that his mother and father died in a car accident that he survived. This is not true. He is not allowed to ask questions about it. Until the character Hagrid appears, like a bumbling fairy godfather, to give him hope, Harry has no way of knowing that any other future is available to him than the dismal life predicted for him by the Dursleys. The magical world of Hogwarts provides Harry, and the children who read the books, with the possibility that the world is not always what it seems to be. In terms of grief and loss, the books repeatedly show children that these are issues that can be talked about, and dealt with, even though it is never easy. Readers also learn that everyone experiences feelings of loss and grief in one way or another, and that surviving these problems can make us compassionate and strong, as well as sad and vulnerable.

Children who have experienced the death of someone close to them often feel different from their peers. They may experience varied reactions from others. Some people may pity them, some people may want to avoid them, and others may view them as brave for carrying on without the loved person. Because of the scar on Harry's forehead, left when Lord Voldemort tried but failed to kill Harry, everyone knows that he is the "boy who lived" through the death of his parents and the attempt on his own life.

At Hogwarts School of Witchcraft and Wizardry, Harry learns that some of his peers have experienced the loss of loved ones. He also learns that many of his peers feel anxiety and sadness for other reasons. For example, even though his friend Ron has grown up as a wizard, and has many siblings at Hogwarts, he sometimes feels like an outsider because his family is poor, and they cannot afford to give him some of the things he wishes for. Although Hermione is one of the most respected students in the school, she sometimes feels like an outsider because both of her parents are Muggles, and because she takes studying and learning more seriously than do most of the other students. Although the focus of the present book is on how to help children and adolescents who are experiencing grief due to the death of someone they cared about, the discussion questions and activities may be able to be applied to wider experiences of grief and loss as well.

J. K. Rowling seems to show a special sensitivity to the anger and hurt that grieving children feel. As has been widely publicized, J. K. Rowling herself experienced the illness, and then death, of her mother at a young age. Shortly before the publication of Rowlings seventh book she noted "My mum died six months into writing (the books), and I think that set the central theme – this boy dealing with loss" (Lawless, 2007, para. 20).

Rowlings has also stated: "I think children are very scared of this stuff (death and loss) even if they haven't experienced it, and I think the way to meet that is head-on. I absolutely believe, as a writer and as a parent, that the solution is not to pretend things don't happen but to examine them in a loving, safe way" (Lawless, 2007, para. 20).

She has personally corresponded with several dying children who were fans of her books and with the parents of children who have died. For example, in January 2000, she sent an e-mail to Catie Hoch, an eight-year-old girl suffering from cancer, who she had heard about. Catie loved Harry Potter, and J. K. Rowling began a correspondence with her, telling her secrets about the fourth book that she was writing. When Rowling heard that cancer had spread to Catie's brain, one month after her ninth birthday, and that she only had a few weeks left to live, Rowling began calling Catie, and reading her the yet unpublished Book 4 over the phone. Three days after Catie died, Rowling wrote to tell Catie's parents that she felt privileged to have had contact with Catie. When Catie's parents established the Catie Hoch Foundation to help young cancer patients, Rowling contributed to it (Gibbs, 2003).

Unit 1
HOGWARTS HOUSES AND OTHER WAYS TO IDENTIFY WITH CHARACTERS

Readers often have favorite characters in the books they love. They may identity with some characters more than others. An easy way to get children and adolescents to talk about themselves, and to describe the person who died, may be to compare themselves and others to the Harry Potter characters. The books contain such a range of creatures, from good to evil, young to old, and magical to muggle, that all readers will have some characters they love to discuss. The books also explore important traits and possessions that shape various characters' identities, like scars, wands, and house affiliation. These things may help children explore their own developing identity, and discuss how grief and loss have shaped or changed their identity.

Theme 2: Harry's Scar*

The jagged scar on Harry Potter's forehead marks him as someone who has experienced, and survived, a great loss. Although grieving children and adolescents do not have a scar to identify their loss, they may find that others identify them primarily as people who have lost someone to death. Their experience of grief and loss may have an important effect on their developing identity. Although scars "heal," they do not leave us.

When people first meet Harry Potter, they often focus on his "fame" for surviving Lord Voldemort's attack. People are impressed with him, and they also feel sorry for him, since he is an orphan. When Ron first meets Harry, he is eager to know about his scar, although later Ron is sometimes jealous of the attention Harry gets for being "the boy who lived." Harry often resents this attention. Sometimes, however, Harry recognizes that people are not always as sensitive as they could be to his loss, or to the loss and grief of others. Because Harry has lost his parents, he can sympathize with the sorrow Neville feels for his institutionalized parents, and for the loss Luna feels about her mother's death. He can also relate to some of the grief and guilt that Harry's godfather Sirius feels about the deaths of Harry's parents.

Harry's scar seems to have positive, as well as negative, aspects. When discussing Harry's scar in Book 1, Ch. 1, Dumbledore says that Harry will have the scar for life, and also that "scars can come in handy." In Book 1, Ch. 2 we learn that the only thing Harry likes about himself is "the thin scar on his forehead." The first question he remembers asking his aunt is how he got the scar. Once he knows the truth about the scar, it becomes a visible reminder of his parents' love for him, as well as a mark of his grief. Harry's scar also symbolizes his own strength and

---

* Note: **Theme 1: The Mirror of Erised** is included in the earlier "How to Use This Book" section.

ability to survive. In Book 2, Dumbledore tells Harry that Voldemort may have put some of his powers into Harry when he gave him the scar, like the ability to talk to snakes through speaking Parseltongue. Harry's scar also acts as a warning beacon to Harry, alerting him through pain whenever Voldemort and danger are near.

The scar therefore makes him unique in ways that are both positive and negative. Experiencing grief and loss is often a complicated process, and can affect children and adolescents in unexpected ways. They may find that they have actually gained some positive traits from experiencing their grief and loss. They may not want to acknowledge that anything positive could come from such sadness. They may need to be reassured that it is ok to change in both positive and negative ways after a loss.

In the real world, while scars may heal so well that they are difficult to see, they are still with us. In an interview with *The Today Show*, after writing Book 7, Rowling said that in her original version of the final line in Book 7, she planned it to be something like "Only those who he loved could see the lightning scar." She decided to change it to the published version lines "The scar had not pained Harry for nineteen years. All was well" (Vieira, 2007, p. 5).

Both of these versions may suggest to children and adolescents reading the books that their grief, like Harry's, will remain with them, but it may not be so intense later in their lives, and perhaps only people that know them well will be aware of their grief. The published version also suggests that, while children will never forget the people they have lost, there may come a time when they can think about them without pain.

Although an important part of Harry's identity in the books is as "the boy who lived," it is not his whole identity. Throughout the books, Harry must try to incorporate the part of him affected by grief and loss with the other parts of his developing self. The following questions and activities can help children, and especially adolescents, explore who they are, and how they can incorporate their loss into their identity in a balanced way.

Possible Discussion Questions

- Why do people in the wizarding world often treat Harry differently once they see his scar?
- When people find out that the child or adolescent has had someone close to them die, do they treat them differently? Discuss.

- What do they wish people would say when they find out that the child or adolescent has experienced a loss?
- How have the losses (through death) that Harry has experienced changed him? How have their experiences of death changed them?
- Does Harry seem to be like his parents in any ways? Do they think that they are at all like the person who has died? If yes, in what ways?
- How would their life be different if the person who died was still alive?
- How would the person who died like to be remembered? How would they like the child or adolescent to go on with their life?
- What are the children's plans for the future? What beliefs/values are most important to them right now?
- If the children had a scar to represent their survival, and the loss of the person who died, what would it look like? Would it have both positive and negative qualities?

Activities

- Ask the children or adolescents to draw a picture/write a story of what they think their life is like now, and what it may be like five years from now.

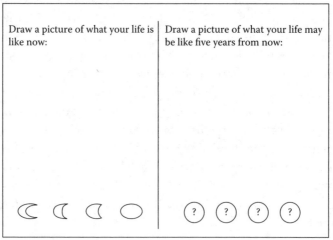

Draw a picture of what your life is like now:	Draw a picture of what your life may be like five years from now:

Worksheet   2

- If they had a scar that represented their grief over the death of their significant person, what would it look like? (Draw and/or write about it.)

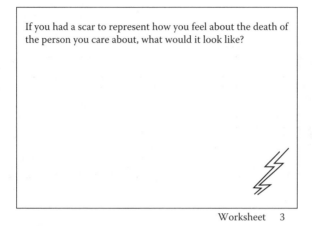

If you had a scar to represent how you feel about the death of
the person you care about, what would it look like?

Worksheet   3

- They could put a picture of their "scar" on a notebook or book bag. That way they can carry the scar as a representation of how grief has affected them, but only share what it means with other people when and if they want to.

Write a story about what your life is like now.

Worksheet   4

> Write a story about what your life will be like five years from now.
> _____
> _____
> _____
> _____
> _____
> _____
> _____
> _____
> _____
> _____
> _____
> _____
> _____
> _____
> _____
> _____

Worksheet   5

Theme 3: The Sorting Hat and Hogwarts Houses

A helpful way to get children and adolescents to talk about themselves and the person who died may be to have them discuss which Hogwarts house they believe they and the person who died would be placed in. At the beginning of each school year, new students are divided into the four houses of Hogwarts School by the Sorting Hat. The students are divided according to their characteristics and talents. When it is Harry's turn to be sorted, the Sorting Hat sees so many different strengths in Harry that it has trouble deciding which house to put him in. Harry pleads not to be put in Slytherin, so the Sorting Hat places him in Gryffindor.

The Sorting Hat sings a new song each year, telling the students about the characteristics of the four houses and the history of Hogwarts School. The songs are found in Book 1, Ch. 7, Book 4, Ch. 12 and Book 5, Ch. 11. We find out that the people placed in Ravenclaw have "wit and learning," the people in Hufflepuff are "just and loyal," those in Gryffindor are "brave at heart," and those in Slytherin are "cunning folk."

The following discussion questions and activities deal with how we can help children to explore the positive and negative characteristics of themselves and of the person who died.

Possible Discussion Questions

- If they could place the person who died in a Hogwarts House, which one would the child or adolescent place them in?
- What characteristics and talents of the person who died made them place that person in the house they chose? Did they consider any other house? Why or why not?
- What house would they place themselves in and why? Would it be the same house or a different house from the person who died? Why or why not?
- If the person who died got to choose what house they wanted to be placed in, what house would they choose?
- If the person who died could place the child or adolescent in a house, what house would they place them in and why?
- How are the houses different from one another? How are the houses the same as one another?
- If they were able to create a new fifth house, what would the new house's name be? What type of students would be placed in the new house and why?

Activities

- Have children draw a picture of the house they feel the Sorting Hat would place them in and the person who died in, or have adolescents write a description of what house they and the person who died would be placed in.
- They could take an online test that will "sort them" into a Hogwarts house on sites like http://www.personalitylab.org/tests/ccq_hogwarts. htm (this is a detailed test fit for older children or adolescents) or http:// www.timidity.org/tests/sortinghat.html (a quick test, but better for older children) or http://www.wizardingworld.com/games/sortinghat.htm (a quick test that could be read to younger children). These are not official Harry Potter sites.

If the person who died could place you in any Hogwarts House, where would they place you? Draw a picture of yourself in that house:

In which Hogwarts House would you place the person who died? Draw the person in that house:

- Make a sorting hat. This could be done by decorating a Halloween costume hat, or by making a cone shaped hat out of paper, and decorating it.

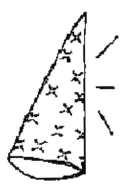

- Write a poem that the hat might sing about where it would place the child or the person who died, and why.

> If the person who died could place you in any Hogwarts House, where would they place you? Write a story about why they would place you in that house.
>
> _____
> _____
> _____
> _____
> _____
> _____
> _____
> _____
> _____
> _____
> _____
> _____
> _____
> _____
> _____
> _____
> _____
> _____
> _____

Worksheet   8

If you could place person who died in any Hogwarts House, where would you place her or him? Write a story about why you would place her or him in that house.

_____
_____
_____
_____
_____
_____
_____
_____
_____
_____
_____
_____
_____

Worksheet   9

Theme 4: Favorite Character

As readers enter the world of Harry Potter, they often find themselves identifying with certain characters more than others, or simply liking certain characters more. Discussing the traits of the characters children identify with, or like, can be another way to help children talk about themselves and the person who died.

Possible Discussion Questions

- Which of the characters in the Harry Potter books does the child or adolescent think is most like him or her? Why?
- Which character is most like the person who died? Why?
- Which characters do they like the most? Which character do they think the person who died would like the most? Why?

Activities

- Ask the child or adolescent to draw a picture of the character they like or identify with most, and the character the person who died would have liked or identified with most.

- Suggest that they search for an online test that asks them questions about their personality, and then tells them which character they are most like.
- Make a poster with pictures of the person who died and pictures of the character they think that person is most like, and/or a poster with pictures of the child or adolescent and the character they most identify with or like.

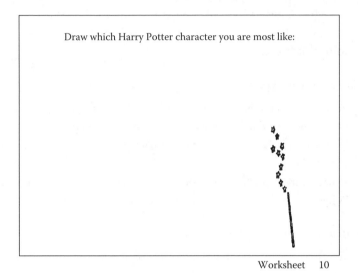

Draw which Harry Potter character you are most like:

Worksheet   10

Draw which Harry Potter character the person who died was most like:

Worksheet   11

Theme 5: Quidditch Team Positions

Many children and adolescents love sports, and love to hear about the wizarding game of Quidditch, which is somewhat of a cross between soccer and hockey, played while flying on broomsticks. Another way to have the children talk about themselves and the person who died would be to ask them which position they would like to play on a quidditch team, and which position the person who died might like to play and why. A description of the various quidditch positions is found in Book 1, Ch. 10, and a brief description is included in the glossary at the end of this book.

Possible Discussion Questions

- What sports does the child or adolescent like to watch or play?
- Did the person who died like to watch or play any sports?
- If they could choose any position to play on a Quidditch team, what would it be?
- What position do they think the person who died might like to play? Why?

Activities

- The children could draw pictures of themselves and/or the person who died as team members playing Quidditch.
- They could write a story about picking their "dream" Quidditch team, including who would be on it, and why.

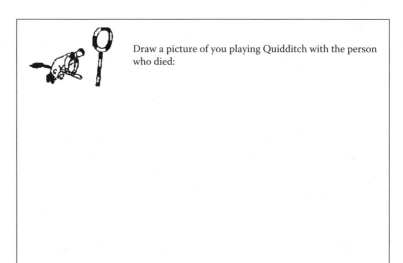

Draw a picture of you playing Quidditch with the person who died:

Worksheet   12

Theme 6: Finding a Wand

Grieving children and adolescents may find that they are often compared to the person who died. Throughout the books we learn that a person's predispositions are important, but that a person's choices in life are at least equally important. This could be a helpful message to grieving children and adolescents: they do need to acknowledge their existing interests and talents, but they can choose different futures than the person who died. They can also choose to do what they think is right for them, even if other people disagree.

When Harry chooses his wand, he finds out that in many ways, the wand chooses its owner. This is done by focusing on the person's strengths. In Book 1, Ch. 5, Mr. Ollivander, the wand shop owner, tells us that he remembers all the wands he has ever sold. He tells Harry that Harry's mother's wand was nice for charm work, and Harry's father's wand was excellent for transfiguration. These wand qualities do seem to predict some of the future traits of Harry's mother Lily and his father James. We find out in later books that his father did become very good at transfiguration, and was able to turn himself into a stag. We also find out that before Lily died, she was able to perform an ancient spell that saved Harry's life, and temporarily destroyed Voldemort. We learn that she was a charming person; Professor Lupin says she helped him when he needed it most, and Professor Slughorn tells Harry that everyone liked his mother. In Book 5, Ch. 28, we even see that Lily defended the difficult-to-like Professor Snape when he was a teenage student being teased by Harry's father.

Harry has a lot to live up to. He is constantly told that he looks like his father, but has his mother's eyes. While he likes being compared to his famous parents, and he is upset if anyone criticizes them, being constantly compared to anyone is difficult to deal with. When Harry's wand "finds him," we see that the match is obvious; indeed fireworks actually go off (Book 1, Ch. 5)! But at that point he learns from Mr. Ollivander that his wand has a phoenix feather in it from the same bird that gave a feather for Voldemort's wand. From that time on, Harry sees that he shares qualities not only with his parents, but also with the wizard who killed his parents. In Book 2, Ch. 18, Harry tells Dumbledore that Tom Riddle (Voldemort's given name) told him that they have strange likenesses in common. This disturbs Harry. Dumbledore confirms that Harry and Voldemort have certain things in common: "His own rare gift, Parseltongue—resourcefulness—determination—a certain disregard for rules…", yet the Sorting Hat placed Harry in Gryffindor, instead of in Voldemort's house Slytherin, because that was Harry's choice (Book 2, Ch. 18, p. 333).

When Harry finds out that he may be like Voldemort in some ways, he is very upset. It helps him to have Dumbledore talk to him and point out that these aspects of his identity are not all bad. In Book 7, Ch. 35, Harry discovers that the strengths he gained by Voldemort's attempt to kill him as a child now help him to survive as a young adult. Grieving children may also find that, although grief and loss are terrible and difficult things to experience, these experiences may leave them with some strengths they did not have before. They may need to be reassured that this is ok.

Solace says to also see **Theme 2: Harry's Scar.**

Many grieving children may feel that, in a sense, their wand is broken. It may seem like nothing has gone well since the person they cared about died. When characters in the book try to use wands that are not theirs, or broken wands, unfortunate things often happen. In Book 1, Ch. 4, when Hagrid uses what we later suspect is his broken wand to turn Dudley into a pig, he only manages to give Dudley a curly tail.

Both Neville and Ron start out at Hogwarts using wands that are not their own. In Book 1, Ch. 6, we learn that Ron has a "very-battered looking wand" that has a unicorn hair almost poking out the end of it. In Book 1, we also learn that it was the wand of Ron's older brother Charlie. In Book 2, Ch. 5, Ron's wand breaks when he and Harry accidentally fly Ron's dad's car into the Whomping Willow tree on the Hogwarts grounds. Ron feels that his parents will think it is his own fault that his wand broke, so he does not ask them for a new one until Book 3. His broken wand causes him many problems in Book 2. One of the worst problems for Ron was having a curse he meant to send to a boy named Draco Malfoy backfire on him, causing him to cough up slugs for several hours.

Neville has been using his father's wand since he started school. This may be partly why he continues to have so many things go wrong in his some of his classes. For example, he has a very difficult time in his Potions class, because Professor Snape makes him unusually nervous.

Solace says to see **Theme 7: Neville's Wand** and **Theme 56: Who Am I Now?** for related issues.

In Book 7, Ch. 17, Hermione accidentally breaks Harry's wand. Harry feels weakened and vulnerable without his wand. Even when he later comes to possess the powerful Elder Wand, he decides that he only wants to use it to repair his own broken wand (Book 7, Ch. 36).

Grieving children and adolescents are often changed by their grief. They may need to choose a new way to live their lives, in a sense, a new wand. When Ron and Neville just accept that they have to use someone else's wand, or a broken wand, to solve their problems, they are often in trouble. When they turn to their family to help them get new wands, they are able to solve their own problems better. Grieving children and adolescents may not even see how their grief is affecting their ability to solve problems and make decisions. They may need help to function in this new world; one without the person they have lost.

Possible Discussion Questions

- What would the child or adolescent's wand be like (length, wood type, springiness, and magical inside element)? Why? (It may help to read the last six pages of Book 1, Ch. 5, to explore what magical wands are like.)
- What would the wand of the person they are grieving for be like? Why?
- How has their life changed since the person they cared about died?
- Have they changed as a person since the person died?
- Would they have had a different wand before the person died than they have now? Discuss.

Activities

- The child or adolescent could draw a picture of their wand and the wand of the person they are grieving for.
- They could make a wand for themselves by drawing and designing a wand on thick cardboard and cutting it out, or by decorating an unsharpened pencil to appear like they imagine their wand would look.

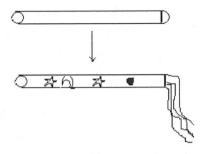

Draw a picture of what you think your wand would look like, and what the wand of the person who died would look like:

Worksheet   13

Write a story about what you think your wand would look like.

_____
_____
_____
_____
_____
_____
_____
_____
_____
_____
_____
_____
_____
_____
_____

Worksheet   14

Write a story about what you think the wand of the person who died would look like.

_____
_____
_____
_____
_____
_____
_____
_____
_____
_____
_____
_____
_____
_____

Worksheet   15

Theme 7: Neville's Wand: Grief for Non-Death Losses

Children and adolescents may experience grief for someone who has not died, but has changed in ways that make them a different person than they were before (i.e., has developed Alzheimer's disease or experienced a brain injury or developed a severe psychological disorder). Like the character Neville, they may not discuss their loss with others and may not get the help they need to deal with their grief. For example, because Neville has experienced the loss of his parents to insanity instead of death, he is not easily identified by others as a grieving child.

From the first time we meet Neville in Book 1, he is clumsy and unsure of himself. He constantly forgets things, and he seems to be bullied by mean students like Draco Malfoy more than the other students. He tells some of the other first-year students that his relatives were relieved when he got his letter to attend Hogwarts, because they were worried that he might not have any magical abilities.

Although Neville is brave, and is even willing to stand up to his friends when he feels they are in the wrong, he often gets into trouble. For example, in Book 3, he loses his list of passwords to get into the Gryffindor tower, which potentially puts all of the students at risk. It is not until Book 4, Ch. 30 that Harry discovers that, in a sense, Neville is an orphan too. After Harry sees a vision, in Dumbledore's Pensieve, of people on trial for cursing Neville's parents, he asks Dumbledore about Neville's parents. Dumbledore seems surprised that Harry does not know, saying "Has Neville never told you why he has been brought up by his grandmother?" (p. 602). Dumbledore tells Harry that Neville's mother and father were driven insane by Death Eaters when Neville was a baby, and they have been hospitalized ever since. Later Dumbledore asks Harry not to tell others about Neville's parents, saying "He has the right to let people know, when he is ready" (Book 4, Ch. 30, p. 604). Grieving children and adolescents also have the right to tell people about their grief in their own way, when they are ready.

By the end of Book 6, Neville has still never directly talked to any students about the "loss" of his parents. Hermione, Ginny, Ron and Harry meet Neville's parents by accident when they are visiting Ron's father in St. Mungo's Hospital in Book 5. Like Dumbledore, Neville's grandmother is surprised that Neville has not told his friends about his parents. She decides that Neville is ashamed of them, but he denies that.

Neville's grandmother describes Neville as a good boy, but says "he hasn't got his father's talent." We don't know why Neville does not discuss his loss with his friends, but throughout the books, he is a very private person. While many students consider Neville to be a friend, he does not seem to have any best friends that he can really confide in.

Until Book 7, he seems to feel both different from, and inferior to, the other students.

From various comments Neville makes throughout the books, it seems that his grandmother has compared him to his brilliant father throughout his life, and Neville has usually been found lacking.

 Solace says also see **Theme 6: Finding a Wand.**

It is not uncommon for children who have experienced a loss through death to be compared to the person who has died. Since our society often "idealizes" people after they have died, this can be a burden for the surviving child. Even if they seem to compare favorably to the dead person, they may worry that they cannot always live up to that comparison, and it could hamper their ability to find their own identity. For example, at the end of Book 5, Ch. 35, Neville's wand shatters as he is fighting the Death Eaters to defend his friends. He tells Harry that his grandmother is going to kill him, because that was his dad's old wand. Rowling writes in Book 1 that a person will "never get such good results with another wizard's wand" (Book 1, Ch. 5, p. 84). After Neville gets his own wand, suited to his characteristics and abilities, he seems to gain confidence. In Book 7, Neville's courage is truly heroic. He spends his year at Hogwarts resisting the Death Eaters that have been teaching at the school. He is able, as only a true Gryffindor could, to pull Godric Gryffindor's sword from the burning Sorting Hat that Voldemort has placed on Neville's head. With the sword, he is able to kill Voldemort's snake and last Horcrux, Nagini.

Possible Discussion Questions

- Why does the child or adolescent think that Neville has not told his friends that his parents were famous Aurors who were driven insane by Death Eaters?
- If Neville told them about his parents, what would they think? What would they say to him?
- Do they ever tell people about the person who has died or changed? Who do they tell? What do other people say? If they told Neville about the person who died or changed, what do they think he would say? Why?
- Do they think Dumbledore or any other adults should talk to Neville about his parents? Would it help Neville? Why or why not?

Activity

• Make or draw a wand for Neville that the child or adolescent thinks would fit him.

Draw a picture of Neville with a wand of his own:

Worksheet   16

Theme 8: Luna Lovegood and Her Mom

Some grieving children or adolescents may identity with Luna. She saw her mother die when she was nine years old. It is difficult for anyone to experience the death of someone they care about, but it may be especially traumatic for a child who already feels different from their peers, and who does not have many friends.

Luna Lovegood is an unusual child. We first meet her in Book 5, Ch. 10. She seems to be quite intelligent, and she is confident in her own opinions, and does not try to conform to the views or fashions of others. However, because she is different, she does not "fit in" well with the other students, and she does not have many friends. In Book 5,

Ch. 38, we find that Luna is often teased by other students, who hide her possessions and call her "loony." Luckily, Luna seems to have a good relationship with her father, and to be happy with herself, even though she knows other people find her to be "odd." Over time, many students come to appreciate her intelligence and loyalty. In Book 7, Ch. 34, when Harry is looking around the Great Hall in Hogwarts for the people that he loves, Luna is one of the people he includes in his list.

Luna is also one of the few Harry Potter characters who seems to believe firmly and confidently in an afterlife. In Book 5, she tells Harry that people who die have gone "behind the veil" and that she knows she will see her mother again. Although Harry does not know whether to believe Luna or not, he finds that his terrible grief over the death of Sirius is lessened a little after hearing her talk about her mother (Book 5, Ch. 38).

Possible Discussion Questions

- Ask the children to list Luna's positive qualities. Ask them to list their positive qualities.
- Why do some students tease Luna? Does anyone tease them? Discuss.
- What helps Luna to deal with the loss of her mother? What helps the child to deal with the death of the person they care about.
- Luna thinks her mother has gone behind a veil, and that she will see her mother again. What do they think happens after a person dies?

Solace says to see related topics in **Theme 12: Seeing the World Differently** and **Theme 13: After Death Beliefs.**

Activities

- The children could write a letter to Luna, advising her about how to deal with people who tease her.
- They could draw a picture of Luna and her mom, before her mom died.

• They could draw a picture of them with the person who died.

Draw a picture of Luna and her mom:

Worksheet   17

Draw a picture of you and the person who died:

Worksheet   18

Theme 9: Names and Their Meanings

Names are such an important part of everyone's identity, both in the books and in the real world. A discussion of the origins of the child or adolescent's name, and the name of the person who died, may be a helpful way for them to share who they are and to discuss the person who died. Many books, articles, and web sites focus on the meanings of the names Rowling gives to her characters. Children may like to explore the meanings of the names in the books, and discuss which names they like and dislike. They could then share their feelings about their own name, and explore what it might mean, and they could explore the meaning of the name of the person who died. They could also discuss what name they might choose for themselves (whether because of sound or meaning) and what name they might choose for the person who died if they had the choice.

For example, www.angelfire.com (not an authorized Harry Potter site) notes that Ludovic "Ludo" Bagman, the head of the Department of Magical Sports and Games in the wizarding world has a first name Ludovic that is from the Gaelic for "devotee of the Lord," (and we find out he had been accused of being a follower of Lord Voldemort in the past), and his nickname, Ludo, means "I play" in Latin (and he was a famous Quidditch player as a young man). The site traces the first name of Professor Minerva McGonagall to the Roman goddess Minerva, goddess of wisdom and war, and notes that Minerva may also mean "wise" (certainly Professor McGonagall is one of the smartest teachers at Hogwarts). They believe McGonagall is from the Celtic Conegal, meaning "the bravest" (in the books, McGonagall is the head of the Gryffindor House, where students are placed if they are brave).

Several times in the books, people tease people, or make fun of their names, when they don't like that person. In Book 1, Ch. 6, Ron laughs at Draco Malfoy's name when he introduces himself. We also find out several times in Books 5 and 6 that people who don't like Luna Lovegood call her Looney. In Book 6, Ginny Weasley, who is usually nice to others, makes fun of Fleur Delacour's name (calling her Phlegm behind her back) because she thinks Fleur is snobbish and self-centered.

Possible Discussion Questions

- Do they know why they were given the name they have?
- Does the child or adolescent like his or her name? Discuss.
- Does he or she think the person who died liked the child's name? Did the person who died like his or her own name?
- If they could choose any name for themselves, would they keep the name they have or change it? Discuss.
- If they could choose any name for the person who died, what would it be? Why?

Activities

- The child or adolescent could explore the meaning of his or her own name and the meaning of the name of the person who died. Sites like http://www.behindthename.com and http://www.parenthood.com may be helpful resources for this search.

- They could make a poster or picture with their name and its meaning on one side, and the name of the person who died and its meaning on the other side. The poster could include words that characterize the child and the person. They could also take each name, and make an acrostic poem by associating a word with each letter in the name (for example Nick could be N for Nice, I for Intelligent, C for Caring, and K for Kind).

Nick
Means Victory of the People
N ice
I ntelligent
C aring
K ind

Bill
Means Resolute Guardian
B old
I nteresting
L oved
L oud

Theme 10: Favorite Teachers

Children and adolescents who are grieving may find that the adults they would normally turn to for help, like their parents or other adult relatives, cannot always help them.

Solace says to see **Theme 17: When Adults Cannot Help** for related activities.

Teachers can often be an important source of support for children who are experiencing problems in their lives. Harry and his friends, like most children and adolescents, spend a lot of time in classrooms with teachers. Harry's teachers are very important to him. He does not like all of them, but he does turn to many of them for advice and support. Some of his teachers, like

Professor Lupin, spend extra time with Harry outside of class, and help
him to deal with problems he is having in his life. Professor Lupin and
Harry become very important to each other. In Book 7, Ch. 25, Lupin
asks Harry to be the godfather of his infant son Ted, and Harry is
delighted. In Book 7, Ch. 34, when Harry uses the Resurrection Stone
to call upon people who had died to help him, Lupin is included along
with Harry's parents James and Lily, and his godfather Sirius.

It may be helpful for the children and adolescents to discuss who
their favorite teachers have been, and which teachers they feel comfortable talking to about their thoughts and feelings.

Possible Discussion Questions
- Who are Harry's favorite professors? Why?
- Which of the Hogwarts professors do the children and adolescents like
  the best? Why?
- Which teachers does Harry talk to about problems he is having?
- Who are some of their favorite teachers?
- Have they ever talked to any teachers about subjects other than school
  work? Discuss.
- Did the person who died ever talk about their teachers? Discuss.

Activities
- Have the children write a letter to one of the Hogwarts professors telling them about what is going on in the child's life.
- Have the child draw a picture of his or her favorite teacher (maybe with
  his or her favorite Hogwarts professor), and write down something he or
  she would like to tell that teacher.
- If appropriate (and the teacher is supportive and understanding about
  the child's grief) help the child or adolescent to arrange a time to talk to
  a favorite teacher outside of class.

Draw a picture of your favorite teacher: Draw a picture of your favorite Hogwarts teacher:

Worksheet   19

Write a story about your favorite teacher.

Worksheet   20

Write a story about your favorite Hogwarts teacher.
_____
_____
_____
_____
_____
_____
_____
_____
_____
_____
_____
_____
_____
_____
_____
_____

Unit 2
Thestrals and Ghosts: Death in the Harry Potter Books

J. K. Rowling has said that "My books are largely about death. They open with the death of Harry's parents. There is Voldemort's obsession with conquering death and his quest for immortality at any price, the goal of anyone with magic..." (Greig, 2006, para. 9). In her books, although many characters still find death to be a taboo subject, many characters do talk about death. Grieving children and adolescents may be able to relate to the anger, sadness, and confusion that Harry and other characters feel when someone they care about dies. And some children and adolescents who have never lost someone to death in their own "real world" may be able to better understand the grief of others as they cope with their own anguish over the death of the characters in the books.

Theme 11: Talking About Death

Many children may experience death as a Voldemort-like part of their life: the **topic which must not be named.** Harry grew up in a house where no one seems to want to talk about serious issues like death. In Book 1, the only information he has been told about his parents' deaths turns out to be untrue. The Dursleys tell Harry that his parents were killed in a car accident. He is told that he was in the car with them, but survived the accident. When Hagrid appears on Harry's eleventh birthday, Harry finds out that his parents were killed by an evil wizard. Later, at Hogwarts School, Harry finds out that some people are willing to discuss the topic of death, although it is never easy. Throughout the books, Harry finds himself continually drawn to others who have experienced grief and loss in their lives, like Sirius, Neville, Luna, Dumbledore and the school ghosts Moaning Myrtle and Nearly Headless Nick.

After Cedric dies in Book 4, Ch. 32, the other students find it difficult to discuss his death, yet everyone is affected by it. Few people want

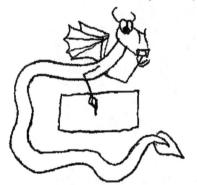

to admit that he was murdered by Lord Voldemort. However, Dumbledore believes it is important to be honest with the students about how Cedric died. He tells the students that he knows some of their parents will be angry with him for telling them this difficult truth.

Solace says to see also **Theme 54: People Don't Know What to Say.**

Possible Discussion Questions

- What do the Dursleys tell Harry about his parents' deaths? Why do they think the Dursleys tell him this? Should they have told him the truth?
- How did they find out that the person they care about died? Do they wish there was some other way that they had been told?

- Who can Harry talk to about serious issues like death? Who can they talk to?
- Are there people that Harry would not or could not talk to about death? Are there people that they would not or could not talk to about death?
- If the child or adolescent needed other people to talk to, who might listen? Is it easier to talk to others who have also experienced grief or loss?
- Cho does not want to talk to anyone except Harry about Cedric's death. Why?
- The Headmaster, Dumbledore, tells the students that some of their parents may be angry that he has told them that Voldemort killed Cedric. Why did he tell them? Was he right in telling them?
- Why are some topics so difficult to discuss, even for adults? What should adults tell children about death?

Activities

- The child or adolescent could draw or list people that they can talk to about grief and loss.
- They could play the card game.

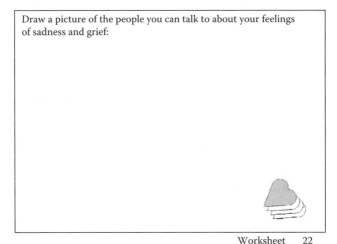

Draw a picture of the people you can talk to about your feelings of sadness and grief:

Worksheet   22

Theme 12: Seeing the World Differently

In Book 5, the only people who can see the magical horse-like creature called a Thestral are those who have seen someone die. In a very real sense, these children now see the world differently than their peers. In the Harry Potter books, they have gained an insight that helps them to solve problems.

Because Harry's peers know that he has experienced grief and loss, they are sometimes freer to share their own feelings of grief with him. In turn, Harry's knowledge that some of his classmates, like Neville Longbottom and Luna Lovegood, have experienced parental loss helps him to connect to them, and understand them, in ways that their other classmates cannot.

Possible Discussion Questions

- Do they think Harry would behave differently if he had not experienced losses in his life? Explain.
- Do they think he would still be friends with Neville and Luna? Explain.
- Do they believe they see the world differently because of their loss? If yes, in what ways?
- Does having someone a person cares about die make that person more sensitive to the losses of others?
- Do they have any friends that have experienced a loss? How are they like or different from that friend?

Activities

- The child or adolescent could draw how a Thestral would look to them.
- They could draw the way they saw the world before and after the death of the person who died.
- They could create a list of things that described their life before the person died, and a list of things that describe their life now. What is the same? What is different? They could paste the list of the way things are now over the list of the way things were before. (If the students write the list of things from the past in dark wide marker, the past list will show through the present list sheet). They could discuss how, even though things have changed, the way things were before are still part of the child's life.
- Have the children look at an object from one side (maybe a three-dimensional sculpture). Have them describe what they see. Have them move around the object and see different parts of it. They could discuss

how people see things differently, depending on where they are standing and depending on what they have experienced in life.

- Read quotes from the Book 5, Ch. 21 about Thestrals and discuss them.

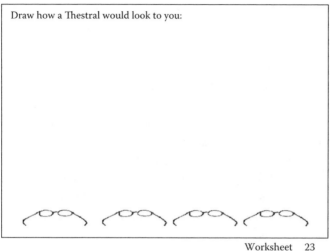

Worksheet   23

Theme 13: After Death Beliefs

Even in the wizarding world of Harry Potter, people are unsure about what happens to someone after they die. In his world, we do know that some people become ghosts, although exactly how that happens remains a mystery. Some of these ghosts include Moaning Myrtle who resides in the girls' lavatory, Professor Binns who is the only ghost teacher at Hogwarts and teaches History of Magic, Nearly Headless

Nick who resides at Gryffindor, The Bloody Baron who resides at Slytherin, The Fat Friar who resides at Hufflepuff, and The Grey Lady who resides at Ravenclaw.

Although readers of Rowling's novels receive interesting pieces of information about what may happen to someone after they die, death remains very much a mystery in the books. In Book 5, Ch. 38, Nearly Headless Nick indicates to Harry that if people choose to become ghosts, they are somehow not as courageous as people who decide to go on to another existence. Some characters, like Luna Lovegood, seem to believe that people go behind a "screen or veil" when they die, and that wizards will see other wizards again in the "afterlife." In Book 7, readers learn that the Resurrection Stone can, in a limited way, bring people back from the dead, but they are not alive and they are still separated from the living. In Book 7, Ch. 35, after Harry talks to the already dead Professor Dumbledore, he asks him if his interaction with Dumbledore is real or if it if happening inside of his head. Dumbledore says, "Of course it is happening inside your head, Harry, but why on earth should that mean that it is not real?" (p. 273).

Possible Discussion Questions

- What have people told the child or adolescent about what happens to a person after they die? What do the children believe?
- Do they know what people in any other cultures/societies believe about the afterlife?
- Do they think that sometimes the topic of death or the afterlife is presented in a frightening way? Discuss.

Activities

- They could draw a picture of what they think has happened to the person who has died.

Draw a picture of what you think happens to people after they die:

??

Worksheet   24

Write a story about what you think happened when the person died

Worksheet   25

- They could put the picture behind some translucent paper, so it can be seen, but is not clear. They could talk about how this may be like the screen that Luna believes people go behind when a person dies.
- The children could create stories telling people what they believe will happen after death.
- Younger children could use puppets to act out what they think happens after a person dies.
- Adolescents could research after-death beliefs in different cultures.

Theme 14: Death Rituals and Mourning

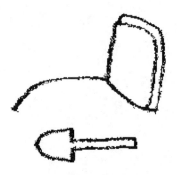

Children and adolescents often attend death rituals such as funerals or memorial services. They may also be part of the preparation for the rituals. However, they may need time to discuss these events in order to fully understand what they have experienced. The discussion and activities for this theme explore ways in which death rituals and ceremonies may be helpful in the healing process for grieving children, adolescents and adults.

When Cedric dies in Book 4, Sirius dies in Book 5, and many characters in the books die in Book 7, there are no funeral or memorial services for any of them. There was, however, a funeral service for Dumbledore after he dies in Book 6 and a short funeral after Dobby dies in Book 7.

When Harry is preparing to go to Dumbledore's funeral in Book 6, Ch. 30, p. 639, like many real children, he is a little apprehensive about what will happen. Rowling writes: "He had never attended a funeral before; there had been no body to bury when Sirius had died. He did not know what to expect and was a little worried about what he might see, about how he would feel. He wondered whether Dumbledore's death would be more real to him once it was over."

In Book 7, Ch. 24, p. 480, after Dobby dies, Harry refuses to use magic to bury him, opting instead to dig Dobby's grave himself. As Harry places Dobby in the grave, "He forced himself not to break down as he remembered Dumbledore's funeral, and the rows and rows of golden chairs, and the Minister of Magic in the front row…He felt that Dobby deserved just as grand a funeral, and yet here the elf lay between bushes in a roughly dug hole."

The only form of ceremony that takes place for Cedric is when Dumbledore addresses the students and faculty of Hogwarts right before the end of the year banquet. Dumbledore remembers Cedric as "a good and loyal friend, a hard worker..." (Book 4, p. 722). Because several of the characters that the readers come to know fairly well throughout the Harry Potter books die, it may be helpful to explore what the grieving child or adolescent think a funeral or memorial service may look like for any of these characters. This may help them to talk about any rituals or ceremonies that were conducted for the person they know who died.

Possible Discussion Questions

- Ask the children or adolescents if they feel it would be important to have a funeral or memorial service for Cedric? For Sirius? For Mad Eye Moody? For Lupin, or Tonks, or Fred? Have them discuss a possible memorial service for any of the characters.
- How would the various funeral or memorial services be different from one another? How would they be the same?
- Are some of the parts of the funeral or memorial service they could imagine for any of the characters the same as the service held for the person who died?
- Are there some parts of their imagined service for any of the characters that are different from the funeral or memorial service held for the person who died? Discuss.
- How might a funeral or memorial service for any of the characters be helpful to their family, friends and the students and faculty of Hogwarts?
- Were there parts of the funeral or memorial service for the person who died that were helpful to the child or adolescent? If they could have included or left out any part of the funeral or memorial service for the person who died, what would it/they be and why?
- Ask the child or adolescent what they felt was beneficial for Harry when he dug Dobby's grave? What did they do or wish they had done in planning or participating in the funeral or memorial for the person who died?
- Ask the child or adolescent what else Harry and his friends might have done for Dobby's funeral? What else could they have said?
- Harry remembered Dumbledore's death and funeral when Dobby dies. Ask the children or adolescents if they remembered other losses in their

lives when the person they cared about died. Do recent losses remind the child or adolescent of how he or she felt when the person died?

Activities

- Have children draw a picture of what a funeral or memorial service may look like for any of the characters, or have adolescents write a description of what would be some of the components of the funeral or memorial service. Have the children "say a few words" they may speak at a funeral or memorial service for any of the characters. Adolescents could write a eulogy for any of the characters.
- The children or adolescents could write an obituary for one or all of the characters who have died in the Harry Potter books.
- Young children could use puppets to act out what a funeral or memorial service might look like for one or all of the characters.
- The child could draw a picture of what the funeral looked like for the person who died.
- The children or adolescents could write a poem or song about one of the characters who died in the Harry Potter books.
- The children or adolescents could create a ritual for one of the characters who died in the Harry Potter books. They could, with the help of the facilitator and other children or adolescents, act out the ritual.

Draw a picture or write a description of what a funeral or memorial service might look like for any of the characters who have died:

Worksheet   26

Theme 15: Grieving the Loss of a Difficult Person

Sometimes the child or adolescent may be grieving for a person who was difficult for them to deal with or was very critical of them. In Book 5, we find that Sirius Black left home at the age of 16 to escape a difficult relationship with his family. His mother was very critical of him. Now, he must live in the house he grew up in, and continually hear the voice of his dead mother (from her painting) criticizing him again. Many people continue to hear the critical voice of a person who has died long after the person is gone. Once a person has died, his or her voice may take on more power, since it can no longer be challenged. Also, many people believe that "we should never speak ill of the dead." The negative comments and behaviors of someone who has died can adversely affect a grieving person's life, especially if the comments and behaviors cannot be acknowledged and examined.

Possible Discussion Questions

- When we first meet Sirius's mother, she is screaming at him: "Blood-traitor, abomination, shame of my flesh!" (Book 5, Ch. 4, p. 78). We find out that she was ashamed of Sirius because he did not believe that pure-blood wizards were better than other people. Ask the child or adolescent if he or she still thinks about problems they had with the person who died? Do they feel bad about things the person who died said to them?
- Ask the child or adolescent who they can be honest with about these issues.
- What would they like to say to the person who died if that person were here today?

Activities

- The children could write a letter to the person who has died, telling them how they feel about that person's past behavior.
- They could advise Sirius about how to deal with his mother's portrait.
- They could write a play about how they would have liked the person who died to have behaved.
- The children could make a list of some of the things that were difficult about the person who died. For each thing listed, the child could write or discuss what they wish had been true about the person who died, or

about their relationship with that person. They could think about how they may be able to get the support and approval that they need now from other people or from themselves.

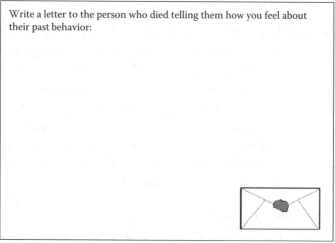

Write a letter to the person who died telling them how you feel about their past behavior:

Worksheet   27

Theme 16: Wishing I Knew You Better

Children and adolescents do not have "equal" relationships with the adults in their lives. The adults who care about them have often known the child since the child was very young, and the focus of their conversations together may have been on the child's interests and activities, not the adults'. When children lose an adult to death, they may begin to realize all the things they never asked the person, and they may hear things about the adult's past that surprise or even upset them. Since the adult is no longer there to explain their life to the child, the child may experience added grief. They have lost not only a relationship, but also the opportunity to know that adult in a deeper way. The child may also be angry or upset that they had not been told certain things about the person before the person died.

Harry finds himself in this position several times in the Rowling novels. He did not have a chance to know his parents at all, and he is upset in Book 5 when he finds out that his father seems to have behaved unfairly toward Severus Snape. In Book 7, Harry is repeatedly reminded of how little he really knows about his mentor, Professor Albus Dumbledore. After Dumbledore's death, Harry realizes that most of their discussions centered on Harry, and Harry had not really thought to ask Dumbledore many questions about himself. Now he has to face the fact that Dumbledore was not perfect. He learns that Dumbledore had been consumed with power and ambition as a young man, and that Dumbledore had played a role in the accidental death of his own sister. Luckily, Dumbledore is magic. Unlike real adults who have died, he can explain his life to Harry even after he has died.

The relationship between Harry and Professor Snape is even more complicated. As Snape is dying in Book 7, Ch. 32, he gives Harry access to some of his memories. Harry realizes only after Snape's death that Snape loved Harry's mother Lily, and that he had been working to help Harry and Professor Dumbledore for most of his adult life. Harry feels grief and remorse that he had believed Snape to be a terrible person.

But in realizing that the adults he has lost are much more complicated and imperfect than he believed, Harry is also able to accept some of his own faults. He is able to realize the things he has in common, not only with his dead parents Lily and James, but also with Dumbledore and Snape. We find out in the Epilogue of Book 7 that these people remain an important part of Harry's life. As an adult, Harry has named his three children after these four people: his eldest son is named James, his daughter is named Lily, and his youngest son is named Albus Severus.

Possible Discussion Questions

- If the child or adolescent could ask the person who died any questions, what would he or she ask?
- Are there things the child found out about the person who died that he or she had not known before? How did that make them feel?

- If they asked the person who died what they were most proud of about their life, and also what they wished had been different, what do they think the person would have said? Why?

Activities

- The child or adolescent could make a scrapbook about the life of the person who died.
- They could make a book for Harry about some of the ways in which Lily and James Potter, Albus Dumbledore and Severus Snape made Harry's world a better place.
- They could write a letter to the person who died, telling them how the child or adolescent feels about what they have found out about the person's life.
- They could list questions they wish they could ask the person who died. An adult could help them explore ways that they could still get answers to some of these questions.

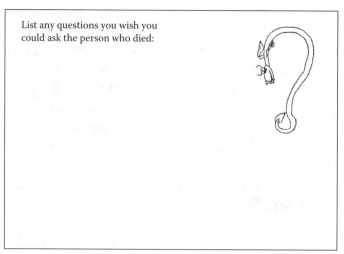

List any questions you wish you could ask the person who died:

Worksheet   28

Theme 17: When Adults Can't Help

When children or adolescents have experienced the loss through death of a significant person, the adults in their life have usually also experienced this loss. The adults may have many problems just dealing with their own grief. They may be unavailable to help the children, or they may be unable to find good solutions to the problems that result from the death. In Book 5, Molly Weasley, who is usually very good at taking care of children, falls apart in front of Harry. She is trying to get rid of a Boggart that is hiding in a writing desk in the drawing room. A Boggart always appears to people as the thing they fear the most. Molly is afraid that people she cares about may be killed by the Death Eaters. When Harry enters the drawing room, he sees Molly sobbing, and he sees what looks like a dead Ron Weasley on the floor. Molly keeps trying to banish the Boggart, but it just keeps turning into different members of her family, all dead. Harry is at a loss as to how to help Mrs. Weasley. Finally, another adult, Professor Lupin, appears and banishes the Boggart and comforts Molly.

Solace says see also **Theme 53: Grief Takes Energy and Time**.

Possible Discussion Questions

- How have adults supported the children or adolescents in their need to grieve? Have adults the child knows ever felt that the child or adolescent should support them in their grief? If so, in what way?
- Is it hard to see adults express their grief (i.e., cry, show sadness and depression)?
- Lupin helped Molly to feel better. Is there someone in the child or adolescent's life who can help the grieving adults they know feel better?

Activities

- Have the children or adolescents write about their parents' or other adults' reactions to the death of the person they care about.
- They could draw a picture or write about grieving adults they know being helped by others.
- They could draw a picture or write about being helped by others.
- The children or adolescents could write a letter to an adult telling them how they feel about the adult's support of them after the death of the significant person.

> Draw a picture or write a story about how other people helped you after the person you cared about died:

Worksheet   29

Theme 18: The Deathday Party

The yearly anniversary of the death of a significant person can be difficult for children and adolescents. They may think about the person, and the death of the person, in a more intense way than at other times

In Book 2, Ch. 8, Nearly Headless Nick asks Harry to his Deathday Party. This is a celebration of the 500th anniversary of the day he died. Harry promises to go, even though it will mean missing the Halloween Feast. Hermione and Ron are also invited to the party and go with Harry.

Possible Discussion Questions

- How is the anniversary of the person's death different from other days of the year?
- On the anniversary of the day the person died, what reminds the child of the person?
- Is there a special way that they and their families remember the person who died on the anniversary of the death?
- Is there a way that the person who died may have wanted people to remember the day of the anniversary of their death?

Activities

- The child could plan a "deathday" remembrance for the person who died. The child could create an invitation to an event to remember the person who died. The invitation could include some activities that the person who died enjoyed (maybe playing a specific card game, watching a favorite movie...).
- The child could write a poem or a song to remember the person or the day they died.
- The child could leave a card for the person at the memorial site or some other special place.

Theme 19: Loss of a Pet

Research has shown that people of all ages can be helped to feel happier and less stressed if they have a pet or interact with friendly animals on a regular basis. The importance of pets is clearly demonstrated in the Harry Potter stories. For example, Harry's owl Hedwig not only helps him with practical matters, like delivering mail, she also keeps him company through the long summers he has to spend with the Dursleys.

Because pets are so important to people, the loss of a pet can be devastating. Other people may not acknowledge this grief, and children especially may be confused and angry about why no one seems to care that their pet is gone. When Ron believes that his pet rat Scabbers has died in Book 3, he wants to blame the loss on others, and he feels that even his friends do not understand how he feels. Hagrid enjoys having many pets in his life. One of his favorite pets was the hippogriff named

Buckbeak. Even though Buckbeak was not ultimately killed in Book 3 (though for part of the book the readers are led to believe that Buckbeak dies), Hagrid's grief over anticipating his loss often overwhelms him. Hagrid loves animals and magical creatures alike, no matter how dangerous or ugly they seem to others.

Solace says see also **Theme 50: True Names for Pets.**

When Hedwig dies in Book 7, Ch. 4, Harry and the other members of

the Order of the Phoenix are at war with Lord Voldemort and the Death Eaters. There is no time to have a memorial service for Hedwig. When Harry tells Hagrid that Hedwig is dead, tears sting his eyes and he thinks, "The owl had been his companion, his one great link with the magical world whenever he had been forced to return to the Dursleys" (Book 7, Ch. 5, p. 67). Although he is not able to have a ceremony to honor Hedwig, he thinks about her several times throughout Book 7.

Possible Discussion Questions

- What was their pet's name, color, or favorite things to do?
- What was their pet's favorite toy to play with?
- What does the child or adolescent miss most about the pet? What are some of their favorite memories of their pet?
- How is the way they feel about their pet the same as the way Hagrid feels about his pets? How is it different?
- How does Harry feel about his owl? What will Harry miss about his owl?

Activities

- Ask the child or adolescent to draw a picture of the pet that died or write a description of the pet.

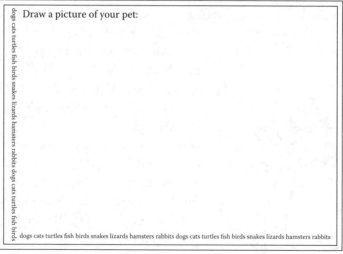

Draw a picture of your pet:

dogs cats turtles fish birds snakes lizards hamsters rabbits dogs cats turtles fish birds

dogs cats turtles fish birds snakes lizards hamsters rabbits dogs cats turtles fish birds snakes lizards hamsters rabbits

Worksheet   30

- The child or adolescent could plan a memorial service for Hedwig. They could write an obituary or eulogy for Hedwig. They could also write one for their pet that has died.

Theme 20: "I'd be furious if it was me!"
Book 5, Ch. 4, p. 66 quote from Hermione

Grieving children and adolescents, as well as grieving adults, may be angry and upset that someone they cared about has died. They may also be angry at the way the death has changed their own lives, and at what seems like the injustice and unfairness of the world. The people around them may not understand their anger or may believe their anger is inappropriate. Even people who do sympathize with their feelings may not know how to help them. The child or adolescent may sometimes push away help. They may believe that if they begin to feel happier, they are somehow betraying or forgetting the person who died.

At the beginning of Book 5, Harry is angry. He has been left to survive the summer after witnessing his classmate Cedric's death, and experiencing his own near death, without any support or advice, let alone grief counseling (!). The adults in his life seem to feel that they are protecting Harry by not telling him what is going on with their fight against Lord Voldemort and his Death Eater followers. But this causes Harry to worry that others see him as weak or untrustworthy. He repeatedly takes out his anger on his friends, yelling at Ron and Hermione, and accusing them of not supporting him. Luckily, they are loyal friends, and they can sympathize with his anger and grief.

Professor Dumbledore refuses to even talk to Harry for most of Harry's fifth year at Hogwarts. Dumbledore fears that if Voldemort finds out how much he cares about Harry, Voldemort will use that knowledge to hurt Harry and others. He realizes too late that this was not the best way to handle the situation, but, like many adults in the real world who are dealing with death and loss, he was trying to do his best in a very difficult situation.

After Harry witnesses his godfather Sirius Black being killed at the end of Book 5 while trying to fight the Death Eaters, Harry is filled with sorrow, guilt and anger. In Book 5, Ch. 37, he is furious with Professor Dumbledore, and he screams at him and even breaks some of Dumbledore's possessions while expressing his anger. After

Dumbledore allows Harry to express his anger, and tells Harry the truth about what has been going on, Harry is able to deal with his grief in a more constructive way. At the beginning of Book 6, Ch. 4, p. 76, Dumbledore tells Harry that he is "pleased and a little proud at how well you seem to be coping after everything that happened at the Ministry. Permit me to say that I think Sirius would have been proud of you." Harry responds that it is hard to realize that Sirius is gone, but that he knows that Sirius would not have wanted him to shut himself away. Harry is still grieving, but he is no longer so angry.

Possible Discussion Questions

- Have they ever been angry about the death of the person they cared about? If so, how have they expressed that anger?
- If Harry had told them that he was very angry with Dumbledore, what might they say to Harry? Have they ever screamed at anyone they have been angry with? Explain.
- When they feel angry, who can they talk to about their anger?
- If they were a friend of Harry's and Harry screamed at them because he was angry and sad, what would they say to him?
- Have they ever yelled at a friend who did not deserve to be yelled at? Explain.

Activities

- The children or adolescents could make a list of things they could do when they feel angry. They could then circle the things that might help them feel better and discuss constructive ways to express their anger.
- They could draw a picture or make a sculpture out of clay to represent what they think their angry feelings might look like.
- They could write a letter to Harry to give him advice about how to deal with his angry feelings.
- They could write a story about what makes them angry and how they behave when they are angry.

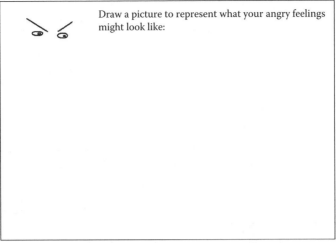

Draw a picture to represent what your angry feelings might look like:

Worksheet   31

Theme 21: Inheritance

Children and adolescents may inherit or be given objects that belonged to the person who died. The objects may be things that they wanted, but they could also be things that they did not want or do not know what to do with. The discussion and activities for this theme explore ways in which inheritance or "things left" to the child or adolescent may be helpful or difficult in the healing process for grieving children, adolescents and adults.

Harry inherits or is given things from several people who have died. Professor Dumbledore gives Harry the Invisibility Cloak that belonged to his father. Sirius Black leaves him his house and all its contents, including the house-elf Kreacher, who is not happy about having Harry as his new master.

Harry, Hermione and Ron all inherit items from Professor Dumbledore. Ron inherits Dumbledore's Deluminator, and Hermione receives a book of fairy tales. Harry inherits Godric Gryffindor's sword and the Snitch he caught in his first-ever Quidditch match. At first none of them can figure out why they were left the items that they inherited. As time goes on, they come to realize the importance of each item and the reason Dumbledore left each of them that specific item.

Possible Discussion Questions

- Ask the children or adolescents why Harry does not want Sirius's house or house-elf Kreacher? Do they think there are items that Harry might wish he had inherited from Sirius? Ask the child or adolescent what she or he has inherited or were given from the person who died. If they could have inherited or been given anything from the person who died, what would it be and why?
- What importance do the item or items they have inherited or been given have to them?
- How did Harry feel about what he inherited or was given? Why?
- What else do they think Harry would have liked to inherit or be given from Dumbledore? Why?
- If they could leave something to someone they love, what would it be and why?
- What did anyone else in their family inherit? Why do they think the person who died left that person what they did?
- What did the person leave them other than items? For example – what was their legacy? Harry is "left" his father's rule breaking behavior and his mother's loyalty. This discussion question may be most useful to older children or adolescents.

Activities

- Have children draw a picture of the item that they inherited or were given.
- Have the children draw or role-play how the item they inherited or wished they had inherited was used when the person who died was alive.
- Have the children create a memory box with items or pictures of items (either photographs or drawings) they inherited or would have liked to inherit. Have them show each item or picture, and tell about its significance to them.
- Have the children write a list of three items they possess that they would like to leave to others when they die. Write why they would leave the item to the person. In a group setting, the child could share his or her list with each other.

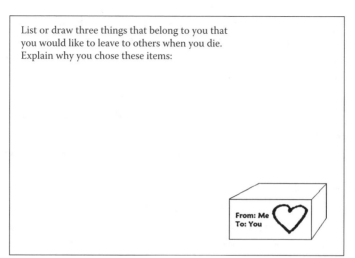

List or draw three things that belong to you that you would like to leave to others when you die. Explain why you chose these items:

From: Me
To: You

Worksheet 32

Theme 22: Fear of Dying

Many grieving children worry that they will die, or that someone else that they care about will die. Thinking about one's own death can be upsetting to people of all ages. Reading about Harry's near-death experience in Book 7, Ch. 34 may help children to feel that death is not such a frightening topic.

In Book 7, Harry finds out that he is an unintentional Horcrux, and Voldemort cannot die as long as Harry lives. Harry goes to the Forbidden Forest. He uses the Resurrection Stone to call for the spirits of people who are important to him and who have died; his parents, Sirius Black and Remus Lupin. The spirits comfort Harry, telling him how brave he is and how proud they are of him and all he has accomplished. Harry approaches what he thinks will be his death with resignation and acceptance. When Voldemort hits Harry with an Avada Kedavra curse, the Horcrux within Harry is destroyed by the killing curse, but Harry, is not killed. He reunites with his friends and fellow schoolmates to defeat the Death Eaters, and ultimately kill Voldemort.

Children and adolescents who are dying may be able to identify with how Harry feels as he enters the Forbidden Forest. They too may feel fear, but be comforted by the people they love. They may come to accept that they are going to die, and they may be able to approach death with less fear. Even though the children or adolescents will probably not have the same outcome as Harry (they will probably not go on to live and defeat what is causing their death), they may be helped to verbalize how they are feeling as they connect with how Harry is approaching what he believes to be his death.

Possible Discussion Questions

- Ask the child or adolescent what feelings Harry has as he enters the Forbidden Forest. Would they, or do they, feel the same way when they think about their own possible death?
- Ask the child or adolescent how their feelings are/would be different from Harry's feelings?
- Harry calls on the spirits of his parents, Sirius Black and Remus Lupin for comfort, as he believes he is about to die. Ask the children who they might call on for comfort and support if they were worried about dying? What might these people – living or dead – say to the child or adolescent that would be helpful and comforting?
- Ask the child or adolescent what they might say to Harry that they feel may be comforting if Harry called to them as he entered the Forbidden Forest.
- Ask the child or adolescent what things Harry's parents, Sirius Black and Remus Lupin said to Harry that would also be helpful to them if they were worried about death?

- Harry feels bad that he is unable to tell the people closest to him about his plans to enter the Forbidden Forest. If Harry was able to tell you about his plans, what might you say to Harry?
- Ask the children or adolescents what they wish Harry would say to them if they told him that they worry about dying.

Activities

- Have the child or adolescent write a list of the things she or he would like to hear if they were worried about dying.
- Have the child or adolescent come up with a list of words that would be helpful for her or him to keep in mind when they think about the end of life.
- Have the child or adolescent paint a picture of what he or she feels an after life looks like. Have her or him explain the painting to an adult or other children or adolescents.

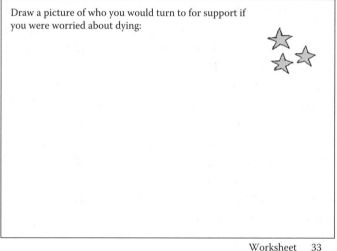

Draw a picture of who you would turn to for support if you were worried about dying:

Worksheet   33

Theme 23: War: "I see them d-d-dead all the time!"
Book 5, Ch. 9, p. 176, said by Molly Weasley

When a country is at war, children and adolescents are affected, whether they know someone who is in the military or not. Stories and photos about the war fill the television news. Children see many pictures of injured and dead soldiers and civilians.

Young children often have trouble distinguishing reality from fantasy. They may be confused about what they see in the news, read in the newspapers, and hear on the radio. Young children may believe that news footage of war is happening right now, or that repeated showings of the same footage are battles or terrorism that is happening again and again (http://www.sesameworkshop.org). Children who have a relative or friend fighting in a war or serving in the military may be reluctant to read or watch the news, or even answer the phone, for fear that they will find out that something bad has happened to someone they care about. On the other hand, they may feel like they have to listen in on adult conversations just to find out what is really happening to people involved with war-time activities.

From the end of Book 4 through the end of Book 7, Harry and his friends are at war with Lord Voldemort and the Death Eaters. At the beginning of Book 5, no one is telling Harry how the war against Voldemort is being waged. His muggle relatives are suspicious when he wants to listen to the news, so he listens to the news and reads newspapers in secret, hoping and dreading that he will find out what Lord Voldemort is doing. Throughout Books 5 and 6, Hermione, Ron and Harry read the *Daily Prophet* newspaper with some anxiety. On a regular basis, they learn that the parents of some of their classmates have disappeared or died in the war with Voldemort and the Death Eaters. Sometimes students at Hogwarts are taken out of school by their parents because of deaths in their families or because parents fear that the school will be attacked. Like adults in the real world, the adults in Harry's world are also upset and stressed about the war, and they are not always able to address the fears and anxieties that the children and adolescents around them are feeling.

Possible Discussion Questions

- How does war change Harry's life and the lives of the other students at Hogwarts?
- How has war changed the child or adolescent's own life?
- If the children or adolescents are upset that someone they care about may be hurt or killed in a war, ask them what their concerns are, and who else they can talk to about their worry.

- If children or adolescents know someone who has been killed or injured in a war, they could talk about what happened and discuss who they and their family can turn to for help with their grief and loss.

Activities

- The child or adolescent could draw a picture showing Harry and his friends fighting Voldemort and the Death Eaters.
- They could also draw a picture of what life is like for Harry and his friends after the war has ended.
- They could draw a picture or write a story about the war that they are presently worrying about.
- They could draw a picture or write a story about what their life will be like when the war is over.

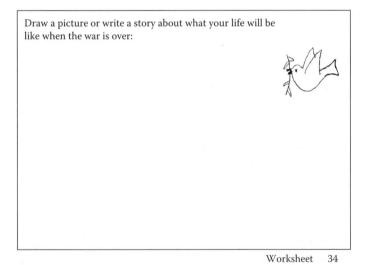

Draw a picture or write a story about what your life will be like when the war is over:

Worksheet   34

Theme 24: The Readers Who Lived

Losing a fictional character "to death" may be as difficult for some readers to deal with as losing a real person that they care about. Yet many people may have trouble sympathizing with the grief someone feels for a fictional character that is dead. In a sense, this is a very "disenfranchised" grief: a grief ignored or invalidated by society (Doka, 2002).

In Books 1-6, readers have had to cope with the loss of three important characters: Cedric Diggory, Sirius Black and Albus Dumbledore.
In Book 7, many important characters die, including characters that
the readers have known for a long time, like Harry's owl Hedwig, his
teacher Professor Lupin and his friends Dobby and Fred Weasley. For
most readers, the amount and type of grief they feel over the loss of
each character corresponds to the grief that Harry feels for the loss
of each person. Readers may be sad to lose Cedric, because he is nice
and he is very young. Young readers may also feel afraid to read that a
character close to their age has died. Readers may be grief-stricken and
confused over the loss of Sirius. He is a complicated character who is
both caring and angry. Readers may feel, like Harry, that they will now
never completely understand Sirius, and so their grief is complicated by
feelings of the injustice of his early death.

Losing Dumbledore may be the most devastating blow that most
readers have experienced in the books. Readers have known Dumbledore for many years, across many books. They know that he is the
only wizard that the evil Lord Voldemort is afraid of. They know that
he loves Harry, and that he believes in Harry. Although they discover,
as the books go on, that Dumbledore is not perfect, he always tries
to be good and kind and wise. The world, both the fictional and the
real, seems safer with Dumbledore in it. Even though Harry believes
Dumbledore really is dead at the end of Book 6, it is not surprising that
many readers refused to accept it.

Sites like http://www.beyondhogwarts.com (including a Dumbledore is not dead analysis) and various Sirius Black memorial sites demonstrate that even fans of the Harry Potter books need help coping with
their grief over the characters who have died. Dave Haber says that he
wants readers to think of his "Dumbledore is not dead" information as
"Half-Blood Prince Therapy."

A July 2005 news article (Readers Respond, 2005) quotes the following reactions from readers of the sixth Harry Potter book:

Madelyne Heyman, age 13: "I was so depressed. I felt like I was
going to cry."

Shelly Blackmore, age 39: "I loved the book. I hated the ending.
There is a death. I sobbed. It was horrible."

George Gelzer, age 10: "freaked out" by the ending. "It's not going
to be the same."

A July 21, 2005 article in the *Boston Globe*, titled "Young Potter Readers Need to Talk, Grieve," describes the shock and grief that many readers felt after reading Book 6. One mother, quoted in the article, said that her usually independent fourteen-year-old daughter asked her mom the day after she finished the book: "Will you be here when I get home at 1 o'clock? I don't want to be alone."

Another fourteen-year-old quoted in the article said: "After I finished, I lay awake and went over and over it in my head until morning... My life is parallel to Harry Potter's. It made me feel really vulnerable. What would I do [in similar situations]? Am I ultimately alone too?"

Many readers need to work through their grief over the loss of characters in the Harry Potter books. Perhaps websites, like the ones noted earlier, can help by giving readers a chance to "honor" the characters, and publicly state how much the characters, even if they are fictional, meant to the reader.

As Dave Haber said on his www.beyondhogwarts.com site on the Dumbledore is Not Dead page:

> "On this site we'll discuss the various clues all throughout Harry Potter and the Half-Blood Prince that will help us get through the tragedy at the end of the book. And while we do this, we will be declaring our love and admiration for Albus Percival Wulfric Brian Dumbledore, and stand together with Harry in declaring that we're 'Dumbledore's man' (or woman), never giving up on him, and never forgetting what he means to Harry, Hogwarts and us."

Many of the activities already described could be used to help readers deal with their grief over the loss of characters they care about.

Solace says see also **Theme 14: Death Rituals and Mourning.**

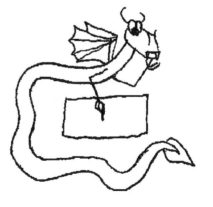

Possible Discussion Questions

- How did you feel when you read that Sirius, Dumbledore or any of the other characters had died?
- Who can you talk to about how the deaths of any of the characters makes you feel?

Activities

- Write an obituary or tribute to Sirius Black or Albus Dumbledore or any of the other characters.
- Draw a picture of the character or characters that you miss the most.

Draw a picture of the character or characters that you miss the most:

Worksheet   35

Unit 3
RIDDIKULUS: DEALING WITH ANXIETIES AND FEARS

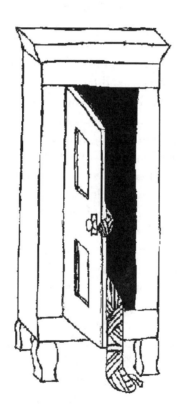

Even in the magical world of wizards and wands, Harry Potter and his friends have many things to worry about, and many fears to deal with. Children may find that talking about how Harry deals with magical creatures like Boggarts and Dementors can help them to think about how they can deal with the challenges in their own lives. Experiencing loss and grief can make people more susceptible to depression and anxiety, especially in stressful situations. Children often need help to deal with their fears, especially those associated with loss and death.

Theme 25: Boggarts, Dementors and Patronuses

In Book 3, Ch. 7, Harry's Defense Against the Dark Arts teacher, Professor Lupin, helps the students overcome Boggarts, creatures that take the shape of the thing the person seeing it fears the most. Lupin points out that Boggarts are less effective when others are with you, because the Boggart gets confused about what to turn into. The way to get rid of a Boggart is to think of some way to make the thing you fear most look humorous, and say the spell "Riddikulus." Each child has a different thing that they fear the most. For example, Ron fears spiders, Neville fears Professor Snape, and Parvati fears mummies. They are all able to imagine the thing they fear as humorous in some way, and that makes their fear, represented by the Boggart, vanish.

In the book *The Optimistic Child*, Martin Seligman (1995) provides ideas about how to "arm" children with strategies to deal with negative thoughts and stressful situations, so that children can decrease their risk of depression. Professor Lupin, who is a werewolf, understands what it is like to feel different. By showing the children how to make Boggarts disappear, he is "arming" them with ways to fight anxiety and depression. However, we find in Book 5, Ch. 9 that even adults sometimes have trouble fighting Boggarts, and there may be times when everyone needs help from others to make their Boggarts disappear.

Lupin's lessons about Boggarts show the Hogwarts students and the readers that the presence and support of others, a sense of humor and a positive outlook can help us deal with the Boggarts in our lives. Dementors, the creatures that guard the Wizard prison Azkaban, drain all the happiness from the humans they are near. We find out in Book 3, Ch. 5, p. 83 that the appearance of the Dementors is associated with death: "There was a hand protruding from the cloak and it was glistening, grayish, slimy-looking, and scabbed, like something dead that had been decayed in water...."

The Dementors cause humans to feel cold and sick, and to only think unhappy thoughts. Because Harry's worst memories, the murder of his parents, are so unhappy, he is more affected by Dementors than other children are. He actually hears Voldemort murdering his mother and then passes out when they are near him. Draco Malfoy teases him about fainting when the Dementors are near, and Harry worries that it shows him to be weak. But Lupin assures him that it has nothing to do with weakness. Harry reacts so strongly to Dementors, Lupin says, "because there are horrors in your past that the others don't have" (Book 3, Ch. 10, p. 187).

Lupin helps Harry to conjure a Patronus to fight the Dementors. A Patronus is a powerful image that can fight off the Dementors, and restore the person's ability to think happy thoughts. At first Lupin feels that Harry is too young to face a Dementor on his own, but when he sees how determined Harry is to fight Dementors, he relents. Some adults may feel that children are too young to face issues of grief and loss on their own, but in a sense, sometimes even young children will need to deal with their grief alone in some ways. The activities and discussion focus on how depression, and certain stressful situations, can make it difficult for people to think positively. They also explore what

"Patronus" children can generate to help them fight off the Dementors in their lives.

Solace says see also **Theme 44: The Key to the Garden**.

Possible Discussion Questions

- What does Harry fear the most? Why?
- Are there things associated with the death of the person they have lost that are scary? Discuss.
- What helps them to overcome their fears?
- Is humor a good way to deal with fear? Does it help to have other people with you when you are afraid? Who/what is the most helpful to the child when they are afraid?
- Are there topics or situations that, like Harry and the Dementors, affect them more than they do other people? Discuss.
- Do they sometimes feel that it is hard to be happy, now that they have lost the person they cared about? Discuss.
- What helps them fight away unhappy thoughts?

Activities

- Have the children draw what a Boggart would look like to them, and then draw a way that they could make the Boggart look humorous.
- Have the adolescents write how a Boggart would look to them and why, and how they could make it look humorous.
- Have the children draw what they think of as Dementors in their life and what their Patronus would look like to chase away Dementors. Or have children or adolescents write about Dementor-like situations in their own lives, and what their Patronus might be.
- Harry's Patronus is actually a symbol used by his father. You could have the child or adolescent discuss, write, or draw a picture to respond to the following questions: If the person you lost could give you a Patronus to fight off unhappiness, what do you think it would be?

The Dementors are creatures that take away all the joy from a person's life, so they can only think sad thoughts. Draw a picture of something that is like a Dementor in your life:

Worksheet   36

Write a story about something that is like a Dementor in your life.

_____
_____
_____
_____
_____
_____
_____
_____
_____
_____
_____
_____
_____
_____
_____
_____
_____
_____

Worksheet   37

A Patronus is something happy and powerful that a witch or wizard can summon to send a Dementor away. What is like a Patronus for you to help you send sad thoughts away?

Worksheet   38

A Boggart is a creature that appears to people as the thing they fear the most. Draw what a Boggart would look like to you:

Worksheet   39

Boggarts lose their power to frighten witches and wizards when the person says the spell "Riddikulus" and thinks of a way to make the Boggart look humorous. Draw how you could make something that is like a Boggart in your life look humorous:

Worksheet   40

Theme 26: Felix Felicis Potion

Grieving children and adolescents may daydream about past times that seemed "perfect" or about how everything would be fine now if only they or someone else had made a different choice in the past. In

Book 6, Ch. 9, Harry has his first potions lesson with the new Hogwarts potions teacher, Professor Slughorn. The professor has brewed various complicated potions as demonstrations for the students. One of the potions is Felix Felicis, which he describes as liquid luck. He tells the students that he will give a small bottle of this amazing potion to the student who does the best potions work that day. Harry follows the suggestions written in the margins of the old potions book that Professor Slughorn has lent him. He produces the best potion in the class, and is awarded with enough of the lucky potion to have what Professor Slughorn says will be "one perfect day" when he drinks it. Professor Slughorn also explains that there are limits to what even something as amazing as the lucky potion can be used to fix. Instead of using the potion to have fun for himself, Harry ends up drinking some of it to solve a problem for Professor Dumbledore, and some of it he gives to his friends to help them protect themselves and others.

We find out in Book 6, Ch. 14, that when Ron thinks Harry has given him the Felix Felicis potion to help him play better Quidditch, he is much better at playing his position as keeper, and the team wins the game. He finds out later that Harry was only pretending to give him the potion. Ron's experience of playing better because he believed he was lucky could apply to the idea of the "power of positive thinking" for grieving children and adolescents. When people are depressed, they often find it difficult to think of positive things. Their belief that nothing is right anymore may lead them to experience more problems and contribute to a vicious cycle of negativity. Identifying positive attributes they have, and small successes in their everyday life, can help them to feel less depressed. This in turn may lead them to experience the events in their lives as more positive.

Solace says see also **Theme 49: The Power of Positive Thinking**.

Possible Discussion Questions

- What would the children do if Harry gave them the bottle of his Felix Felicis potion? Would they keep it all to themselves, or would they share it?

- If the person who died had been given the potion in the past, what do they think the person would have done with it?
- Have they ever felt that they have had a very lucky day? Discuss.

Activities

- Have the children or adolescents write down three things that they like about themselves, and three things that they like about Harry Potter, or one of their favorite Rowling characters.
- Even though Harry has experienced so much grief and loss, he still has happy times in his life. Have the children and adolescents write down three good things that have happened to Harry in the book. Have them write down three good things that have happened in their lives recently.

Things I like about Harry
-he is a good friend
-he is good at flying his broom
-he can make a Patronus

Things I like about Me
-I am a good friend
-I am good at kick ball
-I can make spaghetti

Theme 27: Occlumency and Legilimency

Grieving children and adolescents may find that they can block negative thoughts from their mind when they are busy during the day, but that at night they worry about bad things happening to themselves and others. They may also have bad dreams that reflect the grief and loss they are feeling. Throughout Book 5, Harry has many troubling dreams. Dumbledore believes that Voldemort has a connection to Harry, especially when he is relaxed and vulnerable.

In Book 5, Ch. 24, we find out that Voldemort is skilled at legilimency. This is the ability to extract emotions and memories from the mind of another person. In this chapter, Professor Snape begins to try to teach Harry occlumency, a skill that helps a person fight legilimency by sealing their mind against outside intrusion.

Harry has trouble learning occlumency, partly because he resents having Professor Snape as his teacher and partly because it is a difficult skill to master. To block the connection to Voldemort, Professor Snape tries to get Harry to relax, and to empty his mind of thoughts. Children and adolescents may be able to use relaxation exercises to help them deal with their anxieties when they are trying to sleep or when they are feeling overwhelming anxiety that bad things will happen to themselves or others. These can be the muggle-equivalent of occlumency skills.

Simple relaxation exercises include having the child close their eyes, breathe slowly, and concentrate on one word like "peace" (or wizard!). If their mind wanders from that word, they should not be concerned, but just come back to repeating that word to themselves. Another common technique is to have the child imagine that a weight is going through their body, from the top of their head, down their body and out their feet. As the weight goes through their body, it takes all anxiety and tension with it. They can slowly imagine that it is passing through various parts of their body. It starts on top of their head, and it pushes all the tension down to their eyes, and then their chin, and then their neck, etc. As it goes, it takes all the tension with it.

Possible Discussion Questions

- Harry tries to use occlumency to block Voldemort from entering his mind. Are there ways that the children or adolescents can block troubling thoughts from entering their mind?
- Sometimes Harry has bad dreams that trouble him. Do they ever have bad dreams? Discuss.
- What would they tell Harry if he told them he did not want to have Occlumency lessons anymore?

Activities

- Go through various relaxation exercises with the children or adolescents. Discuss which they like best.
- Have the children write down some of their happiest memories. Discuss how they may be able to focus on these memories when they are feeling bad, having trouble sleeping or have had a bad dream.

Theme 28: Promises: The Unbreakable Vow

Sometimes grieving children and adolescents have made promises to a dying person or have made promises to themselves concerning the dying person. These promises may be impossible for them to keep or cause problems for them to try to keep. Even though promises are not as serious as the Unbreakable Vow from the Harry Potter books discussed here, they may seem magical and powerful to young people. Children and adolescents may believe that something bad will happen if they do not keep their promises concerning someone who has died.

In Book 6, Ch. 2, Professor Snape makes an Unbreakable Vow with Narcissus Malfoy. He vows to protect her son Draco. In Book 6, Ch. 15, Harry overhears Snape reminding Draco that he had vowed to protect him. When Harry tells Ron about this in Book 6, Ch. 16, Ron explains to Harry that if someone breaks an Unbreakable Vow, he or she will die.

Ron tells Harry that when he was about five years old, his brothers Fred and George tried to get him to make an Unbreakable Vow with them. Luckily their father stopped it, but his dad was very angry with Fred and George. He did not believe that children should be making vows with such serious consequences.

In the real world, promises of this sort are often made "in secret," and it may be difficult for the child to discuss them. Even if they do not admit to such promises, it may be helpful for the children to know that it is OK not to keep promises made during a time of grief and loss. The child may need to be reassured that the person who died would want what is best for the child now.

Possible Discussion Questions

- In Books 5 and 6, Harry loses two parental figures who he loves and admires: Sirius Black and Professor Dumbledore. Ask the children what Harry should do if he had promised them something that he cannot fulfill (for example that he would get top grades on all his tests, or that he would be a Prefect?).

- What do they think Sirius or Dumbledore would tell Harry if he could not keep promises he made to them?
- Ask if the children or adolescents have ever made any promises that they had trouble keeping, or could not keep? Discuss.

Activities

- Have the children write a story where Harry made a promise he could not keep.
- They could write Harry a letter to make him feel better if he could not keep a promise he made.
- They could write down what they think the person who died would say to them if they could not keep a promise they made to that person.

Theme 29: All Was Well

Harry's life in the magical world is exciting and filled with wonderful people and amazing adventures. However, it is also filled with terror, loss, sadness and grief. Grieving children and adolescents, may, like Harry, find it difficult to imagine that they will ever find happiness and peace in their future. At the end of Book 6, Harry feels very alone after the death of Professor Dumbledore, and he imagines that his future will be full of hardship and loneliness. In Book 7, he has so many challenges that it is difficult for Harry (and sometimes the readers too!) to imagine a bright and happy future for him. But luckily, in the Epilogue to Book 7, the readers find that Harry has grown up to have a wonderful life. It may be helpful to grieving children and adolescents to read that Harry will be a happy adult. In the Epilogue, the readers find out that Harry has married his love, Ginny Weasley. They have three children, and are actively involved in Harry's godson Teddy's life. Harry is still friends with Ron and Hermione, who have married each other. And he is able to give his youngest son, just starting Hogwarts, the advice and reassurance that he never had as a young boy.

Possible Discussion Questions

- When the children or adolescents imagine their futures, what do they see? If they could dream up a wonderful future for themselves, what would it be like?

- If the person who died could wish for a great future for them, what do they think that person would wish for?
- If Harry could have chosen a "dream" future for himself, do they think it would be like his future in the Epilogue of Book 7? Explain.

Activities

- Draw a picture of Harry as an adult with Ginny and their three children.
- Draw a picture of good things that they imagine could happen in their own futures.
- Write a story about a wonderful future that they might have.

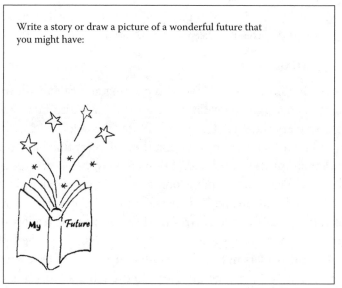

Write a story or draw a picture of a wonderful future that you might have:

Worksheet   41

Unit 4
USING MAGICAL OBJECTS
TO COPE WITH GRIEF

Many of the magical objects described in the Harry Potter novels connect Harry to his dead parents and to other characters in the novels who have died. These magical objects can be used to help children and adolescents explore their grief and connect to and talk about the person who has died.

Theme 30: Remembralls

Children and adolescents are often worried that if they stop focusing on their grief over the person who died, they will forget that person. The following discussion and activities focus on how children can be reassured that they will not forget the person who died, even if they participate in fun activities or don't think about the person everyday.

In Book 1, Ch. 9, Neville receives a remembrall from his grandmother. A remembrall is a small glass ball that tells a person if they have forgotten something. If it turns red when held tightly, it indicates that the person has forgotten something, but it does not tell them what they have forgotten. The concept of a remembrall may be helpful to grieving children. If they record their memories about the person who died in some form, they will not need to worry that those memories will be lost.

Possible Discussion Questions

- If the child could only share five memories about the person who died with someone who never knew them, what would they share?
- If Harry could share memories about Sirius or Dumbledore with someone who never met them, what do you think he might share?
- If they could put memories into a remembrall, so that they could be reminded of the person who died whenever they wanted to, what memories would they include?
- If the person who died made a remembrall to remember their times with the child, what might that person include?

Activities

- Have the children write their memories on small slips of paper and place them in a clear plastic ball (there are many available for Christmas decorating). They could decorate the ball with paint if they wanted to. This will let them create their own remembrall.

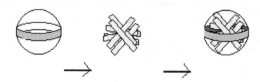

- Another remembrall possibility is to have the child or adolescent write five memories about the person who died, in strips on the other side of stiff wrapping paper, or some other colorful paper. Cut the strips out. Staple the top and bottom of the strips together to form a "ball." If desired, connect a loop of thread or string to one side of the "ball." This will form a colorful ornament that the child could hang up. Their memories will remain inside the ball, but will be hidden unless they want to share them with others.

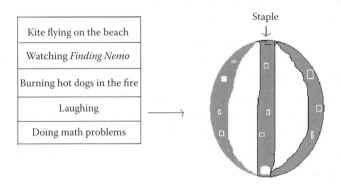

- Children and adolescents could also write their memories about the person who died in a journal or on slips of paper to put into a decorated box.

Theme 31: The Two-Way Mirror

Often grieving children may wish that there was some way they could communicate with the person who died, or they may believe that they can somehow still communicate with that person. They may find it hard to understand and believe that they will really never see or talk to that person again.

In Book 5, Ch. 24, Sirius gives Harry a package, telling Harry not to open it at that time, but to use it if he needs Sirius. It is not until after Sirius has died, in Book 5, Ch. 38, that Harry unwraps the package. He finds an old mirror with a message written on the back by Sirius. It tells Harry that this is a two-way mirror, and that Sirius has the other part. It also says that if Harry says Sirius's name into the mirror, they will be able to see and talk to each other through the mirrors. Harry loudly and clearly says Sirius's name into the mirror, hoping that he can talk to Sirius again, but he cannot, because Sirius is dead. Harry then hopes that Sirius has turned into a ghost, but Nearly Headless Nick tells him that few wizards choose to be ghosts, and Sirius did not choose it. Nick says that he is a ghost because he was afraid to die, so chose to be a ghost instead. Harry feels like he has lost Sirius all over again, because he was so sure that somehow Sirius was not really gone.

Possible Discussion Questions

- If the child or adolescent were Harry's friend, what would he or she tell Harry after he found out that Sirius was not a ghost, and that he could not talk to Sirius through the two-way mirror?
- Have they ever felt that maybe the person who died is not really dead, or has communicated to them in some way? Discuss.
- If Sirius could send a message to Harry when he is feeling so sad about losing Sirius, what do they think Sirius would say? If Harry could really send a message to Sirius, what would Harry say?
- If they could exchange messages with the person who died, what message would they send? Why?

Activity

- Give the children a mirror, and tell them that when they feel that they would like to share something with the person who died, or would just like to write down a feeling that they are having, they can write a message on the mirror in washable magic marker or markers made for writing on glass, and they can later wash it off if they want to.

- Have the children draw a two-way mirror, with a message they would like to send to the person who died on it.

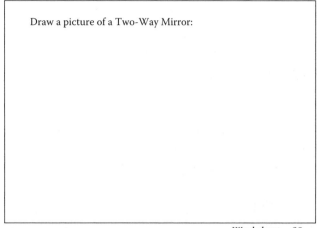

Draw a picture of a Two-Way Mirror:

Worksheet   38

Theme 32: The Pensieve

Sometimes children and adolescents who are grieving may feel that they cannot "turn off" thoughts of their loss to focus on other things. This may be especially a problem when they are trying to get to sleep at night.

Solace says see also **Theme 27: Occlumency and Legilimency.**

In Book 4, Ch. 30, Harry accidentally discovers a pensieve in Dumbledore's office. We find out that a pensieve is a basin that a wizard can place their thoughts in when they feel that their mind is too full of thoughts and memories. In the pensieve, thoughts look like glistening, silvery-white strands. The wizard can examine these strands of their thoughts and memories when they choose to. Dumbledore also uses the pensieve in Books 5 and 6. Even though Dumbledore is the wisest wizard there is, he still has thoughts and memories that he wants to take out of his head sometimes. He does not want to lose these memories, but he wants to have more control over when and how he examines them. In Book 7, Professor Snape shares some of his important memories with Harry by giving Harry his thoughts to examine in the pensieve.

Possible Discussion Questions

- Are there some thoughts or memories that the children or adolescents keeps focusing on, even when they don't want to think about them? Discuss.
- How does it help Dumbledore to put some of his memories in the Pensieve? Is there anything that helps the children or adolescents to stop focusing on memories and thoughts when they want to stop?

Activities

- Have the child or adolescent draw what they think a pensieve would look like or decorate a plastic bowl to look like their vision of a pensieve. Then have them write out (or an adult write out for them) the thoughts or memories they would like to put in the pensieve to think about only when they want to examine these thoughts. This way they will not lose the memories or thoughts, but they may have more control over when they think about them.

Draw what you think a pensieve would look like:

Worksheet   43

Describe what memories you would place in your pensieve:
_____
_____
_____
_____
_____
_____
_____
_____
_____
_____
_____
_____
_____
_____

Worksheet   44

Theme 33: The Portkey

Grieving children and adolescents may find that certain objects or places connect them to the person who died in powerful ways. In Book 4, Ch. 6, we find out that one of the ways that wizards can travel from one place to another is through a portkey. A portkey is an object that, when touched at a prearranged time, can take people from one location to another. It is usually a common object (in Book 4 an old shoe is a portkey, in Book 5 an old tea kettle becomes a portkey), so that Muggles will not touch the objects by accident. The problem with portkeys is that a person could be tricked into touching them and going to some place they don't want to be. This happens to Harry and Cedric when they touch the Triwizard cup together in Book 4, Ch. 31, and end up facing the evil wizard, Lord Voldemort.

Possible Discussion Questions

- If the child and the person who died could have taken a portkey anywhere, where would it be and why? What would the child turn into a portkey?
- Are there objects or events that, like the portkeys in the wizarding world, take the child back to a time with the person who died, or even to the time they did die, or to their funeral? Explain.

Activities

- A portkey is an object that seems common, but actually has great power. The child could think about what object they could carry with them if they wanted to be reminded of the person who died, but that everyone else would think was just a common object. When they touch that object, they could be "taken" to a memory of the person. They could choose or make the object.

Theme 34: Room of Requirement

Grieving children and adolescents may feel more "needy" than other children as they are trying to cope with their loss. It may not be easy for them to explain what they need to help them through this difficult time. Discussing the concept of the Room of Requirement may help them to verbalize the things that they believe would help make their life easier.

In Book 5, Ch. 18, Harry asks the house-elf Dobby if he knows of a room that he and his friends could use to secretly train in defense strategies. Dobby tells Harry about the Room of Requirement. It is a place that appears only when a person needs it and has within it whatever they need for the activity planned. In Book 7, this room provides a place for Neville and the other students who are resisting the Death Eaters to plan their strategies and to hide when needed.

Possible Discussion Questions

- If there was a Room of Requirement in their home or school, what would they want to be in it? Discuss.
- If the person who died could give them a Room of Requirement, what would that person have placed in it? Discuss.

Activities

Take a box, and make it into a Room of Requirement. Decorate the sides of the box as the room walls. Draw, find, or make from clay, objects that might be placed in the box to make the room helpful.

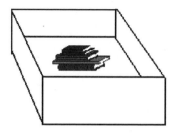

Theme 35: Broomsticks

Children and adolescents often have one or more objects or activities that are important to them and that may help them deal with feelings of depression and sadness. In Book 1, Ch. 9, Harry gets his first flying lesson. He finds that, although he is a natural flyer, some of his friends have more difficulty learning to fly. He feels wonderful when he is flying.

Brooms are very important to Harry in the books. He dreams of owning a wonderful, fast broom, and this actually comes true for him twice, once in Book 1, Ch. 10, and once in Book 3, Ch. 11. He loves his brooms, and takes good care of them. To Harry, a broom represents freedom, adventure, and something he is good at. In Book 7, Ch. 10, Harry finds out that one of his favorite first toys was a small broom given to him by his godfather Sirius Black. Objects like bicycles, rollerblades and skate boards may be a little like brooms to "Muggle" children, representing freedom and adventure.

Possible Discussion Questions

- What is one of the child or adolescent's favorite possessions? Why is this important to them?
- Did the person who died have a favorite possession? Discuss.
- If they could fly anywhere, where would it be? If they could fly anywhere with the person who died, where would they fly?

Activities

- Have the child show or draw their favorite possession, and discuss or write about why it is important to them.
- Draw or make a broomstick. It could be made from a twig with grass or vines tied on the back.

If you could design a flying broomstick for yourself, what would it look like?

Worksheet   45

Theme 36: The Hogwarts Express Train

Children and adolescents who are experiencing grief may wish they could just get away from the situation they are in. Describing fun times they have had, or imagining adventures they could take, may help them take a break from their feelings of loss and sadness. They may like to begin this discussion by imagining where they could take the Hogwarts Express train.

At the beginning of every year, the Hogwarts Express train takes the Hogwarts students to school and it brings them home at the end of the year. The first time the students take the train, they are usually anxious and excited about the new school experiences to come. The train ride is a time for students to spend time relatively unsupervised by adults. The students sit in private compartments that hold four people each, and during the trip a person always come by each compartment to sell candy and cakes to anyone who wants to buy them.

Possible Discussion Questions

- Have they ever taken a train, boat, bus, or plane anywhere? Discuss.
- If they could take the Hogwarts Express somewhere, where would it be?
- What food would they buy from the food seller on the Hogwarts Express? What foods do they think the person who died might have chosen?
- Did they ever take a trip with the person who died? Discuss.

Activities

- They could draw the Hogwarts Express, or make a train out of cardboard
- They could discuss their favorite foods and what the person who died enjoyed eating.
- The children may have fun thinking up new flavors for Bertie Botts Every Flavor Beans.

Draw the Hogwarts Express train:

ALL ABOARD!

Worksheet   46

Write a story about the first ride you might take on the Hogwarts Express.

Worksheet   47

2

Four Other Novels to Help Grieving Children and Adolescents

The four novels included in this section address some of the same topics addressed in the Harry Potter novels, like parental death, death of a peer and death of a pet. In addition, they include themes not addressed by the Harry Potter books, such as the death of a sibling, the belief in prayer, and the power of nature to help relieve feelings of depression.

The four novels work well for children from a variety of different ages, but the themes for each book may work best for children in the age ranges listed as follows:

Title	Author	Suggested Age Range for Theme Questions and Activities
Charlotte's Web	E. B. White	8 years and under
The Secret Garden	Frances Hodgson Burnett	8-12 years
Where the Red Fern Grows	Wilson Rawls	8-15 years
Ordinary People	Judith Guest	15 years and older

Unit 5
CHARLOTTE'S WEB BY E. B. WHITE

Younger children may have many basic questions about death and grief. In *Charlotte's Web*, the character Wilbur the pig asks simple questions about life and death to the spider Charlotte. One of the book's themes concerns how Wilbur's animal and human friends work to keep him from being killed. Wilbur's special friend Charlotte is particularly instrumental in keeping him alive by writing things in her web over Wilbur's pen. She writes words such as "Some Pig," "Radiant," and "Humble." Wilbur's owners and the members of the community are very impressed when they see the words written over Wilbur's pen.

Wilbur is taken to the local fair to be judged. The announcer for the judges says that Wilbur, the famous pig, has brought many valuable tourists to their town. He says that the miracle of the words over the pig's pen has never been explained, and they are from supernatural forces. The announcer gives an award of 25 dollars to Wilbur's owner, Mr. Zuckerman. He also gives Mr. Zuckerman a medal as a special prize. Mr. Zuckerman says that Wilbur will live to a "ripe old age." Everyone is relieved and happy that Wilbur will not be killed.

Wilbur is very grateful to Charlotte for saving his life and for help-ing him to understand death and grief issues. At the end of the book, Charlotte lays eggs while at the Fair and then dies. Wilbur is very sad. Wilbur makes sure that Charlotte's eggs get back to the barnyard safely. When Charlotte's eggs hatch, several of the smaller spiders stay in the barnyard with Wilbur because they are too small to fly away. Wilbur tells them their mother Charlotte was beautiful and loyal to the end. He then introduces the spiders to the rest of the barnyard animals. Wil-bur always remembers Charlotte because, as he says in the last chapter of the book, "It is not often that someone comes along who is a good friend and a true writer. Charlotte was both."

Theme 37: Emotions

Young children may experience many different emotions as they grieve. They may be able to express these emotions to others who can understand and support them, but sometimes they may feel as if they are unable to express their emotions. Wilbur shows many different emotions throughout the book. The different emotions he shows are: happiness, sadness, joy, fear, nervousness, excitement, frustration and anger. He is able to share his feelings with his animal friends in the barnyard.

Possible Discussion Questions

- Have the children talk about the different emotions Wilbur felt through-out the book.
- Have the children discuss which of the feelings that Wilbur experienced are similar to those they have also experienced – especially since the person died.
- Explain to the chidren that all emotions are OK, and that when a person is grieving, she or he often feels all sorts of emotions. Feeling different emotions can be scary and difficult.
- Talk to the children about some of the things Wilbur did when he was feeling different emotions.

Activities

- Have the children act out some of the emotions they have felt. Have them demonstrate what they might do when they are feeling a certain way that might help them feel better.

- Have the children color how different emotions may look if they could see them. Have them explain what they colored and why they chose these colors.

- Give the children modeling clay and have them create what different emotions may look like if they could see them. They may need to be assured that these creations do not need to be anything that looks real. Have them explain their creations.

Theme 38: Feeling Upset

When young children grieve the death of a significant person, they may feel angry and upset. They may be able to find ways to deal with their upset feelings or they may not. When Fern finds out that there is a plan to kill Wilbur, she is very upset. Wilbur's friend Charlotte, who is a spider, is also worried that Wilbur will be killed and creates a plan to keep Wilbur alive. She stays awake all night working and spinning words in her web over Wilbur's pen. The words she spins are, "Some Pig." The people who see the words are very impressed and feel that Wilbur must be very special.

Possible Discussion Questions

- Talk with the children about what upsets them.
- What kind of a plan might the children have to deal with what upsets them?
- Have the children tell about a time when they were upset and they were able to deal with the situation. What happened? Did it help them feel better?

Activities

- Have the children draw a picture of something that upsets them and how they might deal with the situation. They could also write a story or talk about this type of situation.

Draw a picture of something that upsets you and how you might deal with the situation.

Worksheet   48

- Have the children take some modeling clay and form it into something that represents how they feel when they are upset. Have them share the forms with one another and talk about what they formed and why.
- Have the children trace each other's bodies on large sheets of paper. Have the children take the tracing of their own body and color it to represent how they feel when they are upset. They may decide to focus on one part of the body or color the entire body one color or different colors. They could then explain their color choices to the other children in the group.
- Have the children trace each other's bodies on large sheets of paper again. This time have each child color the body to represent how they feel when they are not upset. Have them talk about the colors and discuss how they might get from the upset colors to the colors that are not upset.
- Charlotte decides on a plan to keep Wilbur alive by writing in her web over Wilbur's pen, "Some Pig," so that people who see it will be so impressed that they won't kill Wilbur. Draw a picture of Wilbur and "Some Pig" over his pen. Also, draw a picture of a spiderweb with words in it that describe the person who died.

Fern finds out that there is a plan to kill Wilbur and she is very upset. Charlotte decides on a plan to keep Wilbur alive by writing a positive message about Wilbur in her web over Wilbur's pen. Draw a picture of Wilbur and Charlotte in his pen.

Worksheet   49

Theme 39: Friends

Grieving children can be helped by their friends. In the book, Wilbur and Charlotte are good friends. Not only does Charlotte save Wilbur's life by writing words over his pen in her web, but she and Wilbur have long talks and discuss how they are feeling. Charlotte and Wilbur love one another very much.

Possible Discussion Questions

- Discuss why the children think someone would want to be Wilbur's friend?
- If the children were part of the *Charlotte's Web* story, how would they convince someone that Wilbur would make a good friend?

- Have the children talk about what they liked about the person who died. Have them talk about why the person who died was a good friend – either to the child or to someone else.

Activities

- Have the children draw a picture of the person who died and explain what they liked about that person.

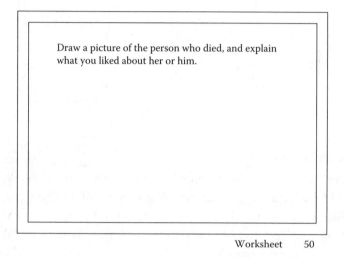

Draw a picture of the person who died, and explain what you liked about her or him.

Worksheet   50

- The children could also write a short story or poem about the person who died.
- Have the children create, draw or write words describing what they learned about being a good friend from the person who died. They could put the creations, drawings or words in a box or bag that they have decorated.
- Have the children create a poster or an advertisement for a magazine about how the person who died was a good friend. They could draw or cut out pictures from magazines to incorporate into the advertisement. The children could also write a script for a radio advertisement that could be read to the rest of the group.
- Wilbur and Charlotte are good friends. They have long talks and discuss how they are feeling. Write down some of the things that they talked about.

Wilbur and Charlotte are good friends. Not only does Charlotte save Wilbur's life by writing words over his pen in her web, but she and Wilbur have long talks and discuss how they are feeling. Write down some of the things that they did or might talk about.

Charlotte said to Wilbur	Wilbur said to Charlotte

Worksheet   51

• Write some reasons why someone would want to be Wilbur's friend.

Write some reasons why someone would want to be Wilbur's friend.

Worksheet   52

Draw a picture of you convincing someone that Wilbur would make a good friend. Think about what you would say.

Worksheet   53

Theme 40: Fun Activities

It may help grieving children to discuss the activities that they like to do, and the good memories that they have of the person who died. In the book, Fern and Avery are friends and enjoy doing things together. They like to swing, catch frogs and pick raspberries and eat them. They also talk about how they want to build a tree house.

Possible Discussion Questions

- Have the children talk about things they enjoyed doing with the person who died.
- Talk with the children about how even though the person has died, the children have memories of things they liked to do with the person.

Activities

- Have the children draw a picture about some activity they liked to do with the person who died.
- The children could write a short story or poem about an activity that they remember. If it is an activity that could be incorporated into a session (such as cooking, knitting, playing a game), the child could teach the other children about the activity.
- Have the children write an Acrostic Poem using the letters from the first name of the person who died, and adding words for activities that the

person enjoyed. (For example: from the name Bill - B is for basketball, i is for ice skating, l is for loving, l is for laughing).

- Have the children create a role-playing scene about an activity that they enjoyed doing with the person who died.
- Have each child create a montage of the things that she or he enjoyed doing with the person who died. Pictures of activities could be cut out of magazines or drawn by the child.

Fern and Avery like to swing, catch frogs, and pick raspberries and eat them. Draw a picture about some activity that you liked to do with the person who died.

Worksheet   54

Fern and Avery like to swing, catch frogs, and pick raspberries and eat them. Write a story about some activity that you liked to do with the person who died.

Worksheet   55

Theme 41: Sadness

Young children often do not understand why people die (it can be difficult for people of all ages to understand why people die). They may feel abandoned and fearful when a person they have loved and depended on dies. Wilbur and Charlotte are very good friends. When Wilbur finds out that Charlotte is going to die soon, he is very upset and pleads with her not to die, but Charlotte says that it is necessary that she die. When Charlotte dies, Wilbur is very sad. Charlotte laid 514 eggs in a sac before she died. Wilbur protects them and makes sure they get back to the barnyard. He has lost a good friend and someone who protected him.

Possible Discussion Questions

- Do the children think Wilbur would have been a friend of Charlotte's if he had known she was going to die soon? Why or why not?
- Have the children tell about things they miss about the person who died.
- Have the children talk about how they felt when they heard that the person was dying or had died. Is this still how they feel or has the feeling changed?

Activities

- Have the child make a "sculpture" out of play dough or clay of something that she or he misses about the person who died. Have the child explain what she or he created to the other children in the group.
- Give the children pieces of play dough or clay and tell then to use it to create how they felt when they heard that the person died. They could also paint how they felt. Tell them that the creation does not need to look like any real object. Have the children explain their creations to the other children.

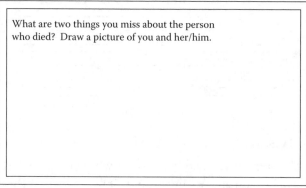

What are two things you miss about the person who died? Draw a picture of you and her/him.

Worksheet   56

> Write what you liked about the person who died
>
> _____
> _____
> _____
> _____
> _____
> _____
> _____
> _____
> _____
> _____
> _____
> _____
> _____
> _____
> _____
> _____
> _____

Worksheet   57

Theme 42: Traits of the Person Who Died

Grieving children may be helped by discussing the special characteristics that are unique to them and to the person who died. For example, Charlotte wrote words about Wilbur in her web: "Some Pig," "Radiant," "Terrific," and "Humble." She wrote the words to show everyone who came to see Wilbur what a special pig he was.

Possible Discussion Questions

- Have the children tell what was special about the person who died?
- Ask the children what words she or he would write about the person who died to show people how special she or he was?

Activities

- Have the children cut words and/or pictures out of magazines that would illustrate what was special about the person who died. Have them create a collage with the words and/or pictures.
- Have the children create a "dream catcher." A dream catcher looks like a spiderweb. The dream catcher's purpose is to catch bad dreams that disappear when the sun come up. Explain that the child's dream catchers are different in that they catch good thoughts and keep them in their hearts forever. After the dream catcher is done, have the children write two or three words that describe the person who died that the child would like to hold in their hearts and secure the words to the dream catcher.

Dream Catcher Instructions

White paper plate, 9"

String or Yarn, at least 48"

Masking tape, pencil, scissors, hole punch

Cut out the center of the plate to the inside edge of the ring. Punch about 12-18 holes around the plate (less if the children are younger and more if the children are older). Wrap masking tape around one end of the yarn. Push the taped end of the yarn through a hole and pull through leaving about 2-3 inches extending out. Start to make a web by pulling the yarn through another hole and crisscrossing the yarn across the center to fill every hole. End the web by bringing the taped end of the yarn back to the first hole and tying to the other end (directions for making the dream catcher was adapted from http://users.safeaccess.com/olsen/njfkcharlotte.html)

- The children could finish the *Charlotte's Web* sentence completion activity:

When Wilbur finds out that Charlotte has died he…

When I found out that the person died I…

When Charlotte dies, Wilbur misses…

Some of the things that I miss most about the person who died are…

Wilbur and Charlotte like each other because…

The person who died and I liked each other because…

The way Fern felt about Wilbur is…

The way I feel about the person who died is…

Some of the barnyard animals who supported Wilbur after Charlotte died are…

Some people who support me now that the person died are…

Templeton likes to…

I like to…

Theme 43: Funeral or Memorial Service

If children are informed about what they will experience at a funeral or memorial service, this type of ritual can be healing for them, just as it can be for adolescents and adults. After Charlotte dies, the animals are sad and miss her a lot; however, they do not have a funeral or memorial service for her.

Possible Discussion Questions

- What are some ways that Charlotte would like to be remembered?
- What are some ways that the person who died will be remembered?
- Have the children talk about the funeral or memorial service for the person who died.
- Was there anything they would have changed about the funeral or memorial service?

Activities

- Have children plan a funeral or memorial service for Charlotte. Have them think of ways to celebrate her life.
- Have each child or pair of children write a simple "eulogy" for Charlotte and read it to the group.
- Have the children write a simple eulogy for the person who died to help the group know the person better.

> When Charlotte dies, there is no funeral or memorial service for her. Draw a picture of what a memorial service would look like. Who would talk about Charlotte, and what would they say?

Worksheet   58

Alone or with another child, write a simple "eulogy" for
Charlotte, and read it to the group.

_____
_____
_____
_____
_____
_____
_____
_____
_____
_____
_____
_____
_____
_____

Worksheet 59

Write a simple "eulogy" for the person who died, and read it to
the group.

_____
_____
_____
_____
_____
_____
_____
_____
_____
_____
_____
_____
_____

Worksheet 60

Unit 6
The Secret Garden by Frances Hodgson Burnett

Grieving children and adolescents may be angry and confused, like the grieving children in *The Secret Garden*. The two main child characters in the book, Mary Lennoy and Colin Craven have both had a parent die. Mary's mother and father die when a cholera epidemic sweeps through the village where she was living in India. She is sent to England to live with her uncle, Colin's father. Colin's mother died when he was very young. Both children are often described as being difficult and rude. Martha, a maid in Colin's house, notes that Mary is "as tyrannical as a pig" and Colin is the "worst young newt as ever was." Their problem behaviors seem, in part, to be a result of their anger at having

their parent(s) die, and at not being included in any decisions being
made about their lives.

Theme 44: The Key to the Garden

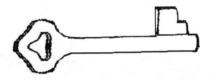

It is often helpful for people who are experiencing depression from
grief to participate in an activity that they enjoy. For example, interact-
ing with nature can help people heal. When Mary is working in her
secret garden, she loses track of time, and she does not dwell on her
problems as much. Her appetite and energy level increase. In Ch. 8, as
she thinks about being outside on the moor she reflects that "…in this
place she was beginning to care and to want to do new things. Already
she felt less 'contrary', though she did not know why" (p. 53).

When her cousin Colin, who has been an 'invalid', starts to spend
time outdoors, he feels better, and he stops obsessing about his health.
In Ch. 26 he explains his feelings about being outdoors in the garden by
saying "I felt so joyful…Suddenly, I felt how different I was—how strong
my arms and legs were, you know—and how I could dig and stand—and
I wanted to shout out something to anything that would listen" (p. 193).

Possible Discussion Questions
- What is something that the child loves to do, or would like to try?
  Discuss.
- What is something that the person who died liked to do or always
  wished they could do? Discuss.
- If the child had found a secret garden, what do they think it would be
  like?

Activities
- Have the child plant something that they would like to plant, or is con-
  venient to plant, indoors or outdoors.
- Go on a walk with the child in a park or woods. If he or she likes to
  identify trees or plants, the child could take a nature book with them,
  and check off the plants that he or she can identify.

- Mary finds a key that enables her to open the door to the secret garden. Draw a key or cut out a key shape from cardboard. On the key, have the child list the places or activities they enjoy.
- Draw a picture of the secret garden.

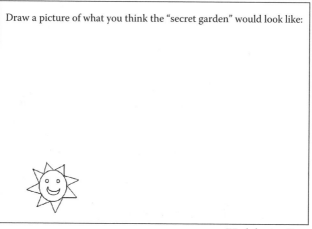

Draw a picture of what you think the "secret garden" would look like:

Worksheet 61

Theme 45: Loneliness

Grieving children and adolescents may feel that no one understands them. This could make them feel that they must handle their grief alone and missing the person who died may make them feel especially lonely.

Mary finds that feeling lonely makes her "sour and cross." She has been so used to people not liking her and not caring about her that when she moves to her uncle's house, Misselthwaite Manor, after her parents die, she does not believe that anyone will be her friend. But as Mary starts to go outside more and interact with new people she sees that she has many friends, both animal, like the robin in the garden, and human, like the children Martha, Dickon and Colin.

Possible Discussion Questions

- Who are the child's friends? Why? Do they wish they had more friends?
- What are some of the things they miss most about the person who died?
- Do they ever feel lonely? Discuss.
- What does Mary do to help her feel less lonely? What can they do to feel less lonely?

Activities

- Have the child draw a picture of Mary's friends.
- The child could draw a picture or write a story about their friends.
- The child could write a letter to a friend to tell them how important their friendship is to the child.

Draw a picture of your friends:

Worksheet   63

Draw a picture of Mary's friends:

Worksheet   62

Theme 46: Difficult Children

Sometimes grieving children may behave rudely or aggressively, and this may push people away from them at a time when they need the help and support of others. Mary and Colin are, in some ways, "spoiled children." When we first meet them, they have not received the friendship and love that they need from others, but they have many material objects, and they have been allowed to yell at adults and tell others what to do.

It helps Mary when the gardener Ben talks to her honestly. In Ch. 4, when they first meet, Mary tells Ben, "I have no friends at all." He responds in his Yorkshire accent that "Tha' an me are a good bit alike... We was wove out of th' same cloth. We're neither of us good-lookin' an' we're both of us as sour as we look. We've got the same nasty tempers, both of us, I'll warrant" (p. 35). No one has ever been honest with her about her behavior before. Reflecting on how she treats others helps her to change.

It also helps Colin to have Mary be honest with him about how rude his behavior seems. She tells him his tantrums are selfish, and that his obsessive worries about his health only make it worse. She is the first person to be honest with him. He wants her to be his friend, so he begins to behave better toward her and toward others around him.

Possible Discussion Questions
- How does the child behave when he or she is angry? Why?
- Has the child ever been rude or mean to anyone? Discuss.
- Was it right for Mary to tell Colin that his behavior was bad? Discuss.

Activities
- Have the children draw a picture of how they behaved sometime when they felt angry.
- Have the children list positive ways to express their anger.
- Have the children advise Mary or Colin on how to express their anger.

Draw a picture of you at a time when you were angry:

Worksheet   64

Theme 47: Sympathy for Others

Children and adolescents are still "egocentric" in many ways. They may not have developed the ability to take another perspective yet or to sympathize with the feelings of others. Grieving children and adolescents may be especially "self-centered." They may have trouble seeing that other people are also affected by the death of the person they have lost, and they may expect that others will be able to "read their mind" and know what they need without being told.

Mary finds that when she starts to develop sympathy for others, she does not feel as miserable. Colin starts to feel better when he stops worrying so much about himself and his health, and starts to take an interest in others and in the world around him.

Possible Discussion Questions

- How has the death of the person they cared about made them feel?
- How do they think it has made other people feel? Discuss.
- How do Dickon, Martha and their mother help Mary in the story?
- How have other people helped the child or adolescent?
- How has the child or adolescent helped others?

Activities

- The child or adolescent could make a list of things that they can do to help others.
- The child could send "get well" cards to sick children in a local hospital.
- The child could volunteer to do an age-appropriate activity, like walking animals at a Humane Society, raking leaves for a neighbor, or running errands for someone who cannot leave their home.

Theme 48: How Could You Die!

It is common for people of all ages to feel angry when someone dies, and to sometimes direct that anger at the person who died. Older children and adolescents may then feel guilty for feeling angry, because they know it was not the dead person's fault. Younger children may not understand that people cannot prevent death, and may feel confused when no one can change the situation.

In Ch. 13 of *The Secret Garden*, Colin shows Mary a picture of his mother, and says, "I don't see why she died. Sometimes I hate her for doing it" (p. 98). Mary does not tell him not to feel this way, but thinks his feelings are "queer." He goes on to list to her all the things that would be better in his life if his mother had not died. Because Colin is in bed all the time with few people to talk to, he feels depressed, and that increases his focus on negative thoughts.

Colin's father has been so affected by his wife's death and his son's ill health that he tries to escape his life by traveling, and he seldom visits Colin. It is not until Colin begins to focus on other activities that he can stop feeling so angry at his mother.

Possible Discussion Questions

- Ask the children why they think Colin sometimes hates his mother for dying. Have they ever felt anger toward the person who died? Discuss.
- What would they tell Colin if he told them that he is angry at his mother for dying?

Activities

- Younger children may benefit from a discussion about how they view death. Research shows that children slowly develop an understanding of important aspects about the concept of death. They may have trouble understanding that death is final and irreversible. They may not understand that it is universal, and that everyone will die. While adults cannot "make" children have a more mature understanding of death, listening to children and trying to answer their questions honestly can help. (See children and grief information at the Association for Death Education and Counseling website: http://www.adec.org/coping/index.cfm.)

- It may be important to assure children that all feelings are acceptable, but that they need to explore positive ways to express their feelings. They could make a list of ways to express their anger that will not hurt anyone, and may help them to feel better. They could draw a picture of some of the positive ways to express their anger, like talking to someone, drawing a picture, singing a song about their anger, etc.

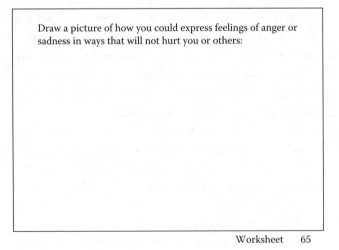

Draw a picture of how you could express feelings of anger or sadness in ways that will not hurt you or others:

Worksheet   65

Theme 49: The Power of Positive Thinking

When people are grieving, their thoughts are often focused on what they have lost and why they are sad. Negative thoughts are a symptom of depression and can also increase feelings of depression. Therapeutic approaches that ask people to challenge their negative thoughts (such as cognitive-behavioral therapy) have been shown to help both children and adults feel less depressed.

Much of Colin's "cure" in *The Secret Garden* depends on him believing that he will get well. After Mary tells him in Ch. 17 that many of his physical problems are just caused by "hysterics," and gets him interested in the secret garden she has found, Colin begins to focus on getting better. He begins to believe that thinking he will get better, and the "power" found in the garden are magical forces that are making him better. In the same way, when Mary begins to believe that she can be likeable, people start to like her. Many of the wonderful changes that happen to the characters in the book seem to depend on the "power of positive thinking!"

Possible Discussion Questions

- Ask the children why thinking about positive things instead of negative things helps Colin and Mary in the story.
- Ask the children what they are thinking to themselves when they feel bad. Discuss how they could challenge their negative thoughts and replace them with more hopeful thoughts.
- If they met Colin at the beginning of the book, when he is focusing on how ill he is and how he may die, what advice would they give to Colin?

Activities

- Have the children make a list of negative thoughts that they have about their life and a list of positive thoughts that they have. Discuss how they can decrease their negative thoughts.
- Have the children make a list of four things they like about themselves. Tell them that when they feel sad or lonely, they could say those things to themselves. If it seems that the children may have low self-esteem, they could say the positive things to themselves every morning or every night.
- Have the children draw a picture of Mary and Colin at the beginning of the book, when they are unhappy, and then at the end of the book, when they are happy.

Draw a picture of Mary and Colin at the beginning of the book, when they are unhappy:

Draw a picture of Mary and Colin at the end of the book, when they are happy:

Worksheet 67

Four things I like about myself:

Worksheet 66

Unit 7
Where the Red Fern Grows
by Wilson Rawls

Having a pet has been shown to help people feel happier and be healthier. Losing a pet can be as difficult for some children and adolescents as losing a person they care about.

In this novel, Billy saves for two years to buy two hound dogs that he can hunt with. Billy spends most of his waking hours with the dogs, and Billy's parents and sisters grow to love the dogs almost as much as Billy does. When the dogs die, Billy is devastated.

Theme 50: True Names for Pets

A helpful way to start a discussion with a child whose pet has died may be to explore how the pet got its name and any nick-names the pet had. In Ch. 6 of *Where the Red Fern Grows*, Billy believes that "fate" helped him name his dogs. While he is bringing his puppies home, he goes over possible names in his mind. Just as he is getting discouraged over not finding the right names, he looks up and sees that a large heart has been carved in the white bark of a sycamore tree. Two names are carved in the heart: Dan and Ann. The name Dan appears much larger and bolder looking than the name Ann, which is very neat and even. Since his female puppy was much smaller than his male puppy, Billy decides that these are the perfect names, so he calls the male Old Dan and the female Little Ann.

In the book, it turns out that these names are prophetic. Old Dan is always more bold and impulsive than Little Ann. She is the smart one, who can be counted on to do every job she is assigned correctly. Together they balance each other out, and their love and protection of each other follows them to their deaths.

Possible Discussion Questions

- Ask the children or adolescents to describe how their pet got their name, and any nicknames the pet had.
- Ask the children or adolescents to describe the "personality" of their pet, and some of the things they miss most about the pet.
- If Billy told them about how sad he was when his dogs died, what would they say to him? Would they have any advice for him?
- When Billy's dogs die, his whole family is sad. Who else is sad that their pet died?

Activities

- They could write a poem about their pet.
- They could make a scrapbook containing pictures and drawings of their pet.
- They could draw a picture of a happy memory of them spending time with their pet.

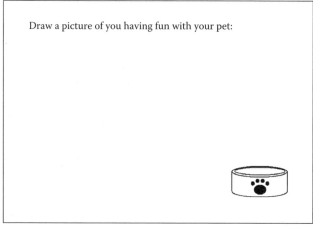

Draw a picture of you having fun with your pet:

Theme 51: Accidental Death

Accidents are the number one cause of death for people between the ages of one and twenty-four (http://www.nlm.nih.gov). When a death is accidental, survivors of the dead person may dwell on how the death could have been prevented. This may lead them to feel guilt and anger about the death.

In *Where the Red Fern Grows,* there are two brothers who often visit Billy's grandfather's store. These boys are poor and they like to make bets. One day they bet Billy that his dogs cannot catch a raccoon that they call the "ghost coon" because it seems to disappear into thin air when it is being hunted. Billy accepts the bet, and goes out hunting with the two boys.

In Ch. 13, the boys get into an argument about who has won the bet. One of the brothers starts to beat Billy, and a hound dog that belongs to the brothers gets into a fight with Billy's two dogs. In all the commotion that follows, one of the brothers, Rubin, falls on an ax and dies. Billy runs home to get help from his parents.

Rubin's family is part of an isolated group of people who live up in the hills. They have a private funeral for Rubin that the rest of the community does not attend. Billy feels bad. He has bad dreams and does not want to go hunting. He feels better after he secretly goes up and puts flowers on Rubin's grave.

Possible Discussion Questions

- How would the children feel about the accidental death of Rubin if they were Billy? Have they known anyone who died accidentally? Discuss.
- If Billy told them that he felt guilty about Rubin's death, what would they tell him? Do they think anyone feels guilty about the death of the person who died? Discuss.
- Billy feels better after he puts flowers on the dead boy's grave. Do they ever visit the grave or memorial place of the person who died? If yes, how do they feel after their visits? If no, would they like to make a visit?

Activities

- If someone they know has died accidentally, they could research how many accidental deaths of that type occur each year. Although it is important not to encourage children to feel guilty or blame others for the death, it may help them to write a report on how future accidents like the one that caused the person's deaths could be prevented.
- The child or adolescent could explore support groups or websites that exist to help people who have lost someone they care about through a specific type of accidental death.

Theme 52: Religion and Death

Research shows that approximately 53% of Americans consider religion to be very important in their lives (http://www.religioustolerance.org/rel_rate.htm). Many people, children and adults alike, turn to their religious beliefs to help them make sense of the losses in their lives, and to give them solace in their grief. Billy and his family are Christians who believe that it will help to pray to God to ask for the things they want. In the first two chapters of the book, Billy pleads with his mother and father to help him buy two hunting dogs. They tell him they cannot afford it. He then tells his father that he only needs one dog, but his father sadly tells him that they cannot even afford one.

In Ch. 3, Billy finds an old sportsman's magazine that advertises "registered redbone coon hound pups—twenty-five dollars each" (p. 18). Billy prays to God to help him get his puppies. He remembers that he has been told that God helps those who help themselves, and so he decides to work and save to get the money for the dogs. After he has saved money for two years he is able to buy the puppies. In Ch. 6, he tells his mother that he will always be grateful that God helped him get his puppies. Throughout the book, Billy has many questions about the power of prayer. He wonders if all prayers are answered, and when his prayers are not answered, he wonders what he has done wrong.

When both of his dogs die, Billy stops believing in prayer for awhile, but later he feels better when he imagines that there is a heaven for dogs.

Possible Discussion Questions

- Billy's family is Christian. Is religion important to the children or adolescents and their families? Do they believe in prayer?
- Billy believes that heaven exists, even for his dogs. What do they think happens to people or pets after they die?

Activities

- Draw a picture of their view of the afterlife.
- Research what different religions believe about what happens to people after they die.

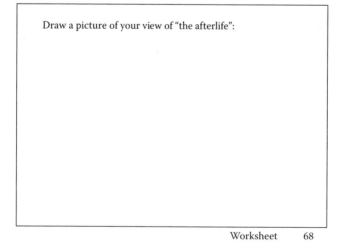

Draw a picture of your view of "the afterlife":

Worksheet   68

Unit 8
ORDINARY PEOPLE BY JUDITH GUEST

This novel may be especially helpful to grieving adolescents. It focuses on the grief that seventeen-year-old Conrad and his family feel after the accidental drowning of Conrad's older brother Buck in a boating accident. When we meet Conrad at the beginning of the novel, it has been over one year since the accident. Conrad has already attempted suicide to try to end the pain and guilt he is feeling over Buck's death.

Conrad's parents, Beth and Calvin, are coping with their grief over Buck's death, and their guilt about Conrad's suicide attempt, very differently. Calvin, whose own mother had died when he was a child, thinks that talking about grief and seeing a psychiatrist can help. Beth believes that she has successfully handled her grief without talking about it. She wants to travel and keep busy, so that the past is not "hanging over her head." Conrad is torn between feeling guilty and sad about his brother's death, and angry at his mother over her lack of support for him through this difficult time.

Theme 53: Grief Takes Energy and Time

The lives of children and adolescents are interrupted by the death of someone they care about. They may miss out on things that are important to them in order to attend the memorial services, and then face their own grief and the grief of those around them. For example, because of Conrad's depression (and subsequent suicide attempt) over his brother Buck's death, he has had to repeat a year of high-school because he did not take his final exams his junior year. Although Conrad never complains about having to repeat a grade, this change in Conrad's life increases his self-consciousness about his brother's death and his own suicide attempt.

Older children and adolescents may feel, or be made to feel, that their sorrow over missing an important game, party, ceremony or school event is unimportant in the face of the death of someone they care about. They may not share, or be validated when they share, continuing feelings of loss over changes in their life that originate with the death. They may also be made to feel guilty for the way other people worry about how they are handling the death of the person they cared about. For example, in Ch. 3, Conrad's grandmother informs him that his father has been very worried about him after his suicide attempt. She says, "If you knew the strain that man was under these past months, the money was nothing, compared with the strain, my heart went out to him, I can't tell you." Conrad feels like screaming "then don't!" (p. 15).

Possible Discussion Questions

- What things changed in Conrad's life after the death of his brother Buck? What changed in the adolescent's life after the death of the person they cared about?
- Do they think Conrad ever feels angry with his brother for dying? Discuss. Do they ever feel angry with the person who died? Discuss.

- Conrad's parents do not agree on the "best" way to help Conrad and themselves deal with their grief. How is his mother's view about this different from his father's view?
- How have people in their life dealt with grief? What advice has anyone given them about how to cope with their grief?

Activities

- What advice might they give to grieving adults who complain that their young teenage son or daughter wants to go to a dance or a ball game only a week after the death of a family member?
- They could imagine that they are an advice columnist. Conrad writes to them to ask for advice on how to deal with his grief. He tells them that he has felt so depressed and guilty about his brother's death that he attempted to kill himself last year. He was hospitalized for some months, and now is home and back at school. He still worries that he will feel overwhelmed by his grief again. What could they suggest to him?
- They could write an educational pamphlet for teenagers containing five things to remember when a person is grieving.

* * * * * * * * * * * * * * *Five Things to Remember When You Are Grieving* By ───────	1. 2. 3.	4. 5.

Worksheet 70

Theme 54: People Don't Know What to Say

Adolescents may feel that many people avoid talking to them or say insensitive things to them after they have experienced the death of someone they care about. Conrad thinks people have trouble talking to him because they don't know what to say about his brother's death or his own suicide attempt. Conrad is not sure how or when to tell new people about his loss.

In Ch. 12, when his new friend Jeannine asks him if he has any siblings, he says he does not, and she says he is lucky. Later, in Ch. 18, Jeannine tells Conrad that she has learned about his brother Buck's death and Conrad's suicide attempt. She says she is sorry for asking about his siblings. He wishes he had told her before, but he did not know how to bring it up. She tries to smooth things over.

"There are worse things," Jeannine says, still looking at her hands. "People do worse things than that."

"Yeah."

He wants to help her through the awkwardness of the moment, but it comes out rudely, as if he is cutting her off (p. 141).

In Ch. 3, Conrad's swimming coach says insensitive things to him about the treatments he has had for his depression. The coach asks Conrad if he had shock treatments, and when Conrad says yes the coach says: "I'm no doctor, but I don't think I'd let them mess around with my head like that." Conrad is angry, but he tries to remind himself that he has never hit it off with the coach, even before his brother died. When Conrad is discussing the coach with his psychiatrist Dr. Berger in Ch. 9, Dr. Berger says: "Sometimes people say stupid things. They feel like they gotta say something, you know?"(p. 73).

Possible Discussion Questions

- Do they think that people ever feel uncomfortable around them because they have lost someone to death? Discuss.
- What do they say when people ask them about the death?
- Do they feel more comfortable talking to some people about their feelings of loss and grief than other people? Explain.
- If Conrad were their friend, and he told them that he felt bad for telling Jeannine that he had no siblings, what would they tell him? Why?

Activities

- If they find it difficult to answer the questions that people have about the death, or to tell people that they don't want to talk about it, they could brainstorm ways that they could respond to people. They could write down these possible responses and even practice them out loud if they wanted to.
- They could write letters to people who have said things they thought were helpful (or insensitive) to them about their grief and loss. They could send the letters to these people if that seemed appropriate.
- They could write a poem or short play about how they feel when people talk to them about the death.
- They could design an educational unit to be shared with teachers, students and other people about helpful things to say and do for people who are grieving.

Theme 55: If Grief Was a Color

Adolescents are just beginning to think abstractly. This often leads them to obsess about abstract concepts, like "the meaning of life" and "what happens after you die." These are fascinating issues that have no correct answer, and so they provide infinite ground for speculation. Adolescents who are grieving may be especially at risk for "over-obsession" about topics related to death and dying. It may help them to verbalize their views about grief and death by having them do the following activities where they are asked to picture grief and death in a variety of creative ways. These could also be used as beginning lines for poems students could write about death or grief.

Possible Discussion Questions

- Are there songs or stories related to death and grief that they like or find interesting? Discuss.
- Do they sometimes feel like they think about death-related issues too much? Explain.

Activities

- They could answer the following worksheet questions about grief and death and discuss them.
- They could use one of the lines they complete as the starting line of a poem or song.

- They could write their answer to complete the grief and death sentences on the inside of Post-it type notes, and paste the notes on top of each question. They could decorate the top of the Post-it notes to create a collage. Example:

| | If death was a animal | If death was a song | If death was a color |

Paste decorated note on statement
square with answer on back of note

| If death was a season | If death was a flavor | If death was a sound |

If death was a color it would be _____.

If death was an animal it would be _____.

If death was a song it would be _____.

If death was a flavor it would be _____.

If death was a season it would be _____.

If death was a sound it would be _____.

If death was a building it would be _____.

Worksheet   71

If grief was a color it would be _____.

If grief was an animal it would be _____.

If grief was a song it would be _____.

If grief was a flavor it would be _____.

If grief was a season it would be _____.

If grief was a sound it would be _____.

If grief was a building it would be _____.

Worksheet 72

Theme 56: Who Am I Now?

Many adolescents already believe that they have an "imaginary audience" that reacts to their appearance and behavior. This makes adolescence a time of increased self-consciousness and egocentrism. An adolescent who has lost someone to death may feel strongly that everyone knows about their loss and is watching to see how they react to it.

In Ch. 5, when Dr. Berger asks Conrad if he feels he is "on stage," he says "...a little, I guess." Throughout the book, Conrad seems to want the approval and attention of others even more than most adolescents. He is also quite sensitive to the feelings of others. He spends a lot of time shopping for Christmas gifts and worries about whether people will like them. He reaches out to an unpopular girl in his math class when she is upset over a test. He tries to keep in touch with a friend from his time in the hospital, and he obsesses about what his new girl friend thinks about him. He appreciates his father's support and tries to please his father. He is angry at his mother's disapproval, but believes he may deserve it.

An important developmental task of adolescence is to develop their identity. It takes time to incorporate the experience of losing someone they care about into that identity process. Part of who they are is someone who has experienced an important loss. Conrad used to be a swimmer like his brother and a more serious student than his brother. Now that his brother is not there, he realizes he doesn't want to swim anymore, but he is not sure what he does want to do.

Possible Discussion Questions

- They could discuss how they think Conrad's life and identity have been changed by his brother's death, and how their life has been changed by the loss of the person they cared about.
- They could discuss what they see as their strengths, and what goals they have for themselves in the near future.
- If the person who died was an adult, they could try to find out what that person was like at their age.
- They could discuss how Conrad is similar to, and dissimilar from, his brother Buck. They could discuss how they are like and not like the person who died.

Activities

- The adolescent could list Conrad's positive and negative qualities and their own positive and negative qualities.
- They could try to predict what Conrad may be doing five years from now, and what they may be doing five years from now.

3

Games

Sometimes children can discuss their feelings more openly in the context of a "game." This section contains two game units. Unit 1 contains game cards and game rules for a "trivia pursuit" type of game using the Harry Potter books. As children play the game and answer the questions, they will also be asked to answer questions that may help them to reflect on their feelings of grief and loss.

Unit 2 contains word completion stories (somewhat like "mad lib" games), and a story based on "Solace the Story Dragon" that can be used as a coloring book or a "draw the story" book.

The games in this section could be adapted for use with a variety of books.

Unit 9
WIZARD CHALLENGE GAME RULES AND GUIDELINES

There are many ways to use the game cards included in this unit to help children discuss grief and loss issues while also playing a game. The following are two different game versions to play with the cards (and possibly a ball). Readers may want to use their own variations.

Game 1: Levitate and Prophesize

Materials Needed:
   Trivia/Discussion cards
   Small, soft ball
   Paper and pencil or pen

Directions:
   Before the game begins, have each child write his or her name on a slip of paper, and put their names in a bowl (or Sorting Hat!). The game leader and children will decide whether they want to keep points, and if so, by individual or by team. If points are to be kept, the game leader will write down each student's name (or team name) on a piece of paper or board to record points. The leader will then draw out a name from the bowl, keeping it secret. The children will begin throwing the ball to each other. After the child whose name has been drawn has caught the ball at least twice (then it is up to the leader) the leader will say stop when that child receives the ball again.

The leader will then ask that child to answer the first trivia question, and if points are being kept, record one point if the child is correct, or none if the child is not correct (or one for the other side if the child is not correct, depending on how competitive everyone wants the game to be!). The leader will then turn over the card, and ask each child in the group to answer the discussion question. (It may be best for children to sit in a circle while answering the discussion questions.) When everyone has had a chance, the leader will draw another name, and the children will start throwing the ball again, using the same rules as before. The game ends when all cards have been used, or when the leader decides to stop.

Game 2: Challenge and Prophesize

(Helpful to use with a smaller number of students, or when a ball cannot be used.)

Materials Needed:
   Trivia/Discussion cards
   Paper and pencil or pen

Directions:
   The leader and children will decide if points should be kept, and if so, individually or by group. The leader will then start by asking a trivia question to one child, and record whether the child got it correct (if points are kept). Then the leader will turn the card over, and each child will answer the discussion question. The leader will then read the next card's trivia question to another child, and continue the game in this same pattern until the group needs to stop or runs out of cards.

Note: **Both versions of the game could be played with just an adult leader and one child.**

Card Game

The cards are formatted so that they can be cut out and folded in half (one half of the card will be the front and one half of the card will be the back). See example below.

Who does Harry live with after his parents are killed?
  a. His grandparents
  b. His aunt and uncle
  c. His older sisters and brothers
	Answer: b. his aunt and uncle
	
	Discussion: Who do you live with and what do you like about living with them?

Front of the card   Fold along dotted line   Back of the card

The cards can also be found in a file on this book's CD. They can be copied on heavy weight paper or card stock, folded and secured together (using tape, glue or staples). Another idea would be to have each part of the card cut out and pasted to the front and back of an index card. The cards can also just be read out loud to children as they appear in the book. The difficulty level of the cards is in random order.

Book One—Game Cards

Less challenging—ask the question and give choices.
More challenging—ask the question without the choices.

Who does Harry live with after his parents are killed?
  a. his grandparents
  b. his aunt and uncle
  c. his older sisters and brothers
	Answer: b. his aunt and uncle
	
	Discussion: Who do you live with and what do you like about living with them?

What kind of an animal is Harry's pet?
  a. a dog
  b. an owl
  c. a cat
	Answer: b. an owl
	
	Discussion: What kind of a pet do you have or wish you had? What do or would you like about this pet?

Who are Harry's best friends?
  a. Hermione and Ron
  b. Malfoy and Snape
  c. Nicholas and Neville
	Answer: a. Hermione and Ron
	
	Discussion: If you were Harry's friend, what would you say to him when he is feeling sad about his parents' deaths?

What is the name for a non-magical person?
   a. wand
   b. Muggle
   c. McGonagall
	Answer: b. muggle
	
	Discussion: If you were magical, what would you do to make the world a better place?

What does Harry's wand have in it?
   a. a phoenix tail feather
   b. an oak branch
   c. a piece of water lily
	Answer: a. a phoenix tail feather
	
	Discussion: If you had a wand, what would it be made of, and what would be the first thing you would do with it?

Who is the headmaster of Hogwarts School of Witchcraft and Wizardry?
   a. Professor Dumbledore
   b. Professor Snape
   c. Professor McGonagall
	Answer: a. Professor Dumbledore
	
	Discussion: Harry looks up to Professor Dumbledore and depends on him for advice. Who do you look up to and depend on for advice and what kind of advice do you receive?

What house is Harry in?
   a. Hufflepuff
   b. Gryffindor
   c. Ravenclaw
	Answer: b. Gryffindor
	
	Discussion: What house would the person who died be in and why?

How does Harry get to Hogwarts school each year?
   a. the Hogwarts Express
   b. an airplane
   c. a magic carpet
	Answer: a. the Hogwarts Express
	
	Discussion: If you could take a magic train anywhere you would like, where would you go, and why?

What are the creatures called whose presence near people takes away all their joy?
   a. the Dementors
   b. the Scabbers
   c. the Seekers
	Answer: a. the Dementors
	
	Discussion: Talk about what could or does take away the joy from your life?

Who kept an important letter away from Harry?
   a. Professor Dumbledore
   b. Hagrid
   c. Uncle Vernon Dursley
	Answer: c. Uncle Vernon Dursley
	
	Discussion: If you were to get an important letter, who would it be from, and what would it say?

What does Harry have on his forehead?
   a. a large bump
   b. a scar
   c. a small picture of his mother
	Answer: b. a scar
	
	Discussion: Harry sometimes feels different from the other children because of his scar. Tell us about what makes you feel different.

When playing Quidditch, what do the players ride?
  a. motorcycles
  b. boxes
  c. brooms
	Answer: c. brooms
	
	Discussion: Harry has a special talent for playing Quidditch. What is your special talent?

Who tells Harry about how his parents really died?
  a. Uncle Vernon Dursley
  b. Hagrid
  c. Ron
	Answer: b. Hagrid
	
	Discussion: How did you find out about the person's death? Who told you? How did you feel?

What does Harry get for Christmas from Mrs. Weasley?
  a. a sweater
  b. a car
  c. a broom
	Answer: a. a sweater
	
	Discussion: What was one gift that you gave to or received from the person who died? Tell us about it.

Who turns from a cat to a person at the beginning of Book 1?
  a. Vernon Dursley
  b. Professor McGonagall
  c. Professor Dumbledore
	Answer: b. Professor McGonagall
	
	Discussion: If the person who died could have turned into an animal, what animal would she/he have been and why?

What did Harry talk with at the zoo when Dudley fell into the cage?
  a. a snake
  b. a rabbit
  c. a giraffe
	Answer: a. a snake
	
	Discussion: If you could talk to just one type of animal, what would it be and what might you say?

How many letters from Hogwarts were delivered to Harry at the Dursleys' house?
  a. one letter
  b. twelve letters
  c. many, many letters
	Answer: c. many, many letters
	
	Discussion: If you could receive a letter from the person who died, what might it say?

Where does Harry buy his school supplies?
  a. Diagon Alley
  b. a grocery store
  c. Target
	Answer: a. Diagon Alley
	
	Discussion: If you could buy a book of magic, what would the title be?

How old was Harry when he was admitted to Hogwarts School of Witchcraft and Wizardry?
  a. 8 years old
  b. 11 years old
  c. 15 years old
	Answer: b. 11 years old
	
	Discussion: Tell about one memory you have of the person who died. How old were you then?

What is the name of the game that Harry plays?
  a. Soccer
  b. Dungeons and Dragons
  c. Quidditch
	Answer: c. Quidditch
	
	Discussion: If you could play Quidditch, what position would you play and why? What position would the person who died play?

What kind of an egg does Hagrid win from a stranger?
  a. a dragon egg
  b. a chicken egg
  c. a turtle egg
	Answer: a. a dragon egg
	
	Discussion: If you had a magical egg, what kind of a creature would hatch out of it?

Who gave Harry Potter the invisibility cloak?
  a. Hermione
  b. Dumbledore
  c. Hagrid
	Answer: b. Dumbledore
	
	Discussion: If you could wear the invisibility cloak, when would you wear it, and what would you see?

What is Hedwig?
  a. a pig
  b. a rat
  c. an owl
	Answer: c. an owl
	
	Discussion: If you could send Hedwig with a message to someone, who would you send the message to, and what would the message say?

What is the name of the three-headed dog who is guarding the trap door in Book 1?
  a. Moody
  b. Fluffy
  c. Attacker
	Answer: b. Fluffy
	
	Discussion: What would you want to be guarded and why?

Ron had Percy's old rat. What was the rat's name?
  a. Scabbers
  b. Carl
  c. Hedwig
	Answer: a. Scabbers
	
	Discussion: If you could have anything you wanted from the person who died, what would it be and why would you want it?

Book Two—Game Cards
(If the children are familiar with Books 1 and 2—mix the cards.)

Less challenging—ask the question and give choices.
More challenging—ask the question without the choices.

What type of creature is Dobby?
  a. a house-elf
  b. a student at Hogwarts
  c. a professor at Hogwarts
	Answer: a. a house-elf
	
	Discussion: House-elves help out witches and wizards. If you were a house-elf, whom would you help, and what would you do?

Why does Harry ride in a flying car to Hogwarts?
  a. He cannot get to Platform 9¾.
  b. He thought it would be quicker than taking the train.
  c. The train was not working so all the students need to arrive in flying cars.
	Answer: a. He cannot get to Platform 9¾.
	
	Discussion: If you could ride in a magical flying car, where would you go?

What creature's cry is fatal to anyone who hears it?
  a. a Boggart's
  b. a cat's
  c. a mandrake's
	Answer: c. a mandrake's
	
	Discussion: If you could have one of the magical creatures from the Harry Potter books as a pet, what creature would you choose and why?

Where does Moaning Myrtle stay?
  a. the girls' dorm
  b. the girls' bathroom
  c. the hallway
	Answer: b. the girls' bathroom
	
	Discussion: If you could live anywhere, where would you live and why?

Polyjuice Potion is used to:
  a. transform people, temporarily, to look like other people
  b. rid Hogwarts of Boggarts
  c. help adults become energetic
	Answer: a. transform people, temporarily, to look like other people
	
	Discussion: If you could be another person for a day, who would you be and why?

What is a Parselmouth?
  a. someone who can talk with unicorns
  b. someone who can talk with others who have died
  c. someone who can talk with snakes
	Answer: c. someone who can talk with snakes
	
	Discussion: If one of the magical creatures or animals from the Harry Potter books could communicate with you, what would it say, and how would you reply?

During Harry's second year at Hogwarts, who is the Defense Against the Dark Arts teacher?
  a. Professor Dumbledore
  b. Professor Lockhart
  c. Hagrid
	Answer: b. Professor Lockhart
	
	Discussion: If the person who died could teach any subject at Hogwarts, what would it be and why?

Who has his five hundredth Deathday Party on Halloween?
  a. Nearly Headless Nick
  b. Dobby
  c. Professor McGonagall
	Answer: a. Nearly Headless Nick
	
	Discussion: How do you remember the day that the person died?

What is Aragog?
  a. a horse
  b. a dog
  c. a spider
	Answer: c. a spider
	
	Discussion: If the person who died could be any animal, what would she/he be and why?

Who does Harry find in the Chamber of Secrets, barely alive?
  a. Ginny Weasley
  b. Mrs. Weasley
  c. Ron Weasley
	Answer: a. Ginny Weasley
	
	Discussion: If you went into another Chamber of Secrets at Hogwarts, what might you find there?

Book Three - Game Cards
(If the children are familiar with Books 1, 2, and 3—mix the cards.)

Less challenging—ask the question and give choices.
More challenging—ask the question without the choices.

What does Harry do to Aunt Marge?
  a. He causes her to swell like a
     balloon and drift up in the air.
  b. He causes her to shrink and finally
     disappear.
  c. He causes her to lose her voice.
	Answer: a. He causes her to swell like a balloon and drift up in the air
	
	Discussion: If you had magical powers, what might you do?

What prison did Sirius Black escape from?
  a. Hogwarts
  b. Azkaban
  c. Erised
	Answer: b. Azkaban
	
	Discussion: Sirius is confined to an actual prison and cannot get away. Is there anything you feel you would like to get away from and why?

When Harry gets on the Knight Bus, what does he say his name is?
  a. Ron Weasley
  b. Sirius Black
  c. Neville Longbottom
	Answer: c. Neville Longbottom
	
	Discussion: Do you ever wish you could be another person? If so, who would you want to be and why?

Who buys a huge orange cat called Crookshanks?
  a. Hermione
  b. Ron
  c. Harry
	Answer: a. Hermione
	
	Discussion: If you could buy a gift for the person who died, what would that present be, and why would you buy it?

If a Dementor comes close to a person, what will be taken away from the person?
  a. Their problems
  b. Their joy
  c. Their physical pain
	Answer: b. Their joy
	
	Discussion: What takes away your joy? Explain.

What will a Patronus shield a person from?
  a. a Dementor
  b. a cold
  c. Aragog
	Answer: a. a Dementor
	
	Discussion: What can help you feel better when you are feeling sad?

What is Buckbeak?
  a. a duck
  b. a mandrake
  c. a hippogriff
	Answer: c. a hippogriff
	
	Discussion: Buckbeak can fly. If you could fly away with Buckbeak, where would you go and why?

What is an Animagus?
  a. a witch or wizard who can turn into an animal
  b. a small bowl of magical powder
  c. an owl
	Answer: a. a witch or wizard who can turn into an animal
	
	Discussion: If the person who died was an animal, what kind of animal would she/he be and why?

Who is Sirius Black?
  a. Harry's brother
  b. Harry's cousin
  c. Harry's godfather
	Answer: c. Harry's godfather
	
	Discussion: Who is one special person in your life? Tell us about her/him.

Who does Professor McGonagall give the Time-Turner to?
  a. Ron
  b. Hermione
  c. Sirius Black
	Answer: b. Hermione
	
	Discussion: If you would turn back time, what time would you go back to and why?

Book Four—Game Cards
(If the children are familiar with Books 1, 2, 3, and 4—mix the cards.)

Less challenging—ask the question and give choices.
More challenging—ask the question without the choices.

What is Ron's new pet after Scabbers? a. a horse named "Scabbers II" b. a pigeon named "Bob" c. an owl named "Pigwidgeon"	**Answer:** c. an owl named "Pigwidgeon" **Discussion:** How are you like an owl? How is the person who died like an owl?
When the Weasley's go to pick up Harry to attend the Quidditch World Cup, Dudley eats one of Fred's sweets. What happens to Dudley? a. His tongue swells up immensely. b. His toes shrink. c. His fingers become as long as the coffee table.	**Answer:** a. His tongue swells up immensely. **Discussion:** If you could create a kind of magical candy, what would happen when someone ate it?
What is a Portkey? a. a key that is used to open a door leading to Hogwarts b. an object used to transport wizards from one spot to another at a prearranged time c. a bottle of butterbeer	**Answer:** b. an object used to transport wizards from one spot to another at a prearranged time **Discussion:** If you could create a Portkey, what object would it be and where would it go?
What does a Pensieve store? a. promises b. silver c. memories	**Answer:** c. memories **Discussion:** What memory or memories would you want to store in a Pensive and why?
Mad-Eye Moody is an old friend of a. Dumbledore's b. Vernon Dursley's c. Hermione's	**Answer:** a. Dumbledore's **Discussion:** Tell us about a friend of yours who you have had for a long time.
The Imperius Curse a. gives total control over a person or creature b. forms a protective shield around the person who uses it correctly c. enables the user to travel from one place to another	**Answer:** a. gives total control over a person or creature **Discussion:** If you could cast an Imperius Curse to help someone, who would you cast it on, and how might you be able to help the person?

What does S.P.E.W. stand for?
  a. Start Printing Everything in White
  b. Students Putting Elves in Wheat
  c. Society for the Promotion of Elfish Welfare
	Answer: c. Society for the Promotion of Elfish Welfare
	
	Discussion: If you could start a society, what would it be called and who would help?

Whose sign is the Dark Mark?
  a. Harry's
  b. Dumbledore's
  c. Voldemort's
	Answer: c. Voldemort's
	
	Discussion: If you could create a "mark" that would warn people of something, what would the sign be, who would it warn, and what would it warn them of?

Rita Skeeter writes for what newspaper?
  a. *Elf Times*
  b. *Daily Prophet*
  c. *Voldemort's Daily Gossip*
	Answer: b. *Daily Prophet*
	
	Discussion: If you could write an article for a newspaper, what would the name of the newspaper be and what would your article be titled?

Which one of Harry's classmates is killed by Voldemort?
  a. Cedric Diggory
  b. Ron Weasley
  c. Neville Longbottom
	Answer: a. Cedric Diggory
	
	Discussion: When Cedric dies, Harry has many different feelings. Tell us about some of the feelings you experienced and may still be experiencing after the person you cared about died. How have these feelings changed over time?

Book Five—Game Cards
(If the children are familiar with Books 1, 2, 3, 4, and 5–mix the cards.)

Less challenging—ask the question and give choices.
More challenging—ask the question without the choices.

What are Harry and Dudley attacked by? a. Dementors b. a Patronus c. a Howler	**Answer:** a. Dementors **Discussion:** The Dementors are very scary creatures. What is scary to you and how do you deal with your feelings?
What does Sirius Black's mother's painting do? a. say nice things to people as they walk into the room b. just hang on the wall c. yell mean things at Sirius and others	**Answer:** c. yell mean things at Sirius and others **Discussion:** If you had a picture of the person who died, what would it say?
Sirius Black's brother Regulus Black used to be: a. a Death Eater b. a muggle c. The Headmaster of Hogwarts	**Answer:** a. Death Eater **Discussion:** Death Eaters are very mean. If the Death Eaters could be as nice as they are mean, what might they be able to do?
When Harry goes to Professor Umbridge's room for detention, he is told to use a quill of hers. What does the quill do? a. cuts the skin of his hand as he writes b. make music c. scolds Harry for his misbehavior	**Answer:** a. cuts the skin of his hand as he writes **Discussion:** If you had a magical quill that could do nice things, what would your quill do?
Umbridge becomes Hogwarts High Inquisitor. What does she do as High Inquisitor? a. ask the students how they are doing b. monitor the Hogwarts educational system c. inquire into how much time it takes the students to get from one class to the next	**Answer:** b. monitor the Hogwarts educational system **Discussion:** If you were the High Inquisitor of something, what would it be, and what would your duties be?

What is the Room of Requirement?
  a. a place where all the students are required to go after lunch
  b. a place where the students go to get their homework done
  c. a place a person can only enter when they have real need of it
	Answer: c. a place a person can only enter when they have real need of it.
	
	Discussion: If you could go to a room and receive what you need, where would the room be and what would you receive?

A Ministry Decree gives Umbridge
  a. a large increase in pay
  b. a retirement party
  c. supreme power over punishments, sanctions and removal of privileges from students
	Answer: c. supreme power over punishments, sanctions and removal of privileges from students
	
	Discussion: If you could have supreme power, what would you do and why?

People who have seen death are the only ones who can see what?
  a. house-elves
  b. Thestrals
  c. muggles
	Answer: b. Thestrals
	
	Discussion: How do you see the world differently, now that you have experienced the death of someone?

Who does Harry have a date with on Valentine's Day?
  a. Rita Skeeter
  b. Cho
  c. Hermione
	Answer: b. Cho
	
	Discussion: Who do you enjoy spending time with and why?

Who is killed in Book 5?
  a. Hermione
  b. Sirius
  c. Cho
	Answer: b. Sirius
	
	Discussion: Harry feels very sad that Sirius was killed. What might you say to him?

Book Six—Game Cards

(If the children are familiar with Books 1, 2, 3, 4, 5, and 6—mix the cards.)

Less challenging—ask the question and give choices.
More challenging—ask the question without the choices.

Who does Narcissa ask to make the Unbreakable Vow to promise to watch over Draco?
  a. Harry
  b. Hagrid
  c. Snape
	Answer: c. Snape
	
	Discussion: If you were to make an Unbreakable Vow to someone, what would that vow be and who would you make it to?

Horace Slughorn decides to take a job where?
  a. as a professor at Hogwarts
  b. as a medical doctor at St. Mungo's Hospital for Magical Maladies and Injuries
  c. the Chairwizard of the International Association of Quidditch
	Answer: a. as a professor at Hogwarts
	
	Discussion: If the person who died could have any job she/he wanted at Hogwarts, what would the job be, and why would she/he want it?

Harry and Ron did OK on their OWLs. How does Hermione do?
  a. poor
  b. alright
  c. excellent
	Answer: c. excellent
	
	Discussion: The OWLs are tests to find out how talented witches and wizards are at certain skills. What do you have a lot of talent in and how high would your score be if you took a test on that skill?

What kind of an injury does Dumbledore have?
  a. a broken leg
  b. one blackened hand
  c. a scratched shoulder
	Answer: b. one blackened hand
	
	Discussion: Dumbledore is secretive about what happened to his hand because he didn't want others to know what had happened. Have you ever had a time when you wanted to be secretive about something? Explain.

Who gives Harry private lessons so he is prepared to face Voldemort?
  a. Professor Dumbledore
  b. Hermione
  c. Professor Snape
	Answer: a. Professor Dumbledore
	
	Discussion: If you could take private lessons from someone to learn what she or he knows, who would teach you, and what would you learn?

The Felix Felicis potion is a. a liquid that makes a person grow tall b. liquid luck c. something that all students must have in order to return to Hogwarts	**Answer:** b. liquid luck **Discussion:** If you had some Felix Felicis potion, when might you use it?
Who was the Half-Blood Prince? a. Professor Snape b. Professor Dumbledore c. Harry Potter	**Answer:** a. Professor Snape **Discussion:** If you could give the person who died a nickname, what would the name be and why would you give them that name?
Who kills Dumbledore? a. Lord Voldemort b. Professor Slughorn c. Professor Snape	**Answer:** c. Professor Snape **Discussion:** When Dumbledore is killed Harry needs to tell Hagrid. If you were Harry, what might you say to Hagrid to tell him of Dumbledore's death?
What are Horcruxes? a. an object in which a person has concealed part of their soul b. a box that has a large picture in it c. a monkey like creature	**Answer:** a. an object in which a person has concealed part of their soul **Discussion:** If you could keep the memory of the person who died alive in an object, what object would it be and what would you like to remember?
Who drinks the emerald liquid in the glowing basin on a small island? a. Lord Voldemort b. Professor Slughorn c. Professor Dumbledore	**Answer:** c. Professor Dumbledore **Discussion:** Harry promises that he will keep giving Dumbledore the emerald liquid even when he didn't want to. What might be a promise that you would make that may be difficult to keep?

Book Seven—Game Cards

(If the children are familiar with Books 1, 2, 3, 4, 5, 6, and 7—mix the cards.)

Less challenging—ask the question and give choices.
More challenging—ask the question without the choices.

Where do the Dursley's go to keep safe? a. into hiding with some wizards b. to the beach with Harry c. to London with Mrs. Fig	**Answer:** a. into hiding with some wizards **Discussion:** Where do you consider to be a "safe place?"
Shortly before Harry leaves Privet Drive for good, what does Dudley do? a. he expresses his gratitude to Harry for saving him from the Dementors b. he gives Harry some of his old cloths c. he tells Harry that he wants to go to Hogwarts and asks how he can get there.	**Answer:** a. he expresses his gratitude to Harry for saving him from the Dementors two years before **Discussion:** What would you like to thank someone for?
What does Ron inherit from Dumbledore? a. a book of fairy tales b. a Deluminator c. a sword	**Answer:** a Deluminator **Discussion:** What is one thing the person who died left you or what is something you would have liked the person to have left you?
When the Order of the Phoenix members escort Harry, how many Harry-look-alike decoys do they create? a. three b. six c. nine	**Answer:** b. six **Discussion:** Harry's friends from the Order of the Phoenix help Harry. Who do you help and how do you help them?
Who accidentally breaks Harry's wand? a. Ron b. Hermione c. Snape	**Answer:** b. Hermione **Discussion:** Hermione feels bad about breaking Harry's wand. What have you felt bad about that you have done—accidentally or not?

When Harry, Hermione and Ron are imprisoned at Malfoy Manor, who rescues them by apparating them to Bill and Fleur Weasley's home?
  a. Dumbledore
  b. Mrs. Weasley
  c. Dobby
	Answer: c. Dobby
	
	Discussion: Dobby always looks out for Harry and keeps him safe. Who in your life looks out for you and keeps you safe?

When Harry goes into the Forbidden Forest to meet Voldemort, what spirits does he call to be with him?
  a. Mrs. Weasley, Mr. Weasley, and Fred Weasley
  b. his parents, Sirius Black, and Remus Lupin
  c. Dumbledore, Dobby, and Hedwig
	Answer: b. his parents, Sirius Black, and Remus Lupin
	
	Discussion: Harry is comforted by what his parents, Sirius Black, and Remus Lupin say to him. Who in your life can you go to for comfort?

Who sent the doe Patronus that led Harry to Gryffindor's sword?
  a. Dumbledore
  b. George Weasley
  c. Snape
	Answer: c. Snape
	
	Discussion: If the person who died was going to send you a Patronus, what would it look like and what would it do?

What does Harry use to fix his wand?
  a. some strong tape
  b. the Elder Wand
  c. Snape fixes it for Harry
	Answer: b. the Elder Wand
	
	Discussion: Harry's wand is very important to him. What item is important to you and why?

At the end of the book we find out that nineteen years after the battle at Hogwarts, Harry is married to?
  a. Ginny Weasley
  b. Hermione Granger
  c. Luna Lovegood
	Answer: a. Ginny Weasley
	
	Discussion: When you think of your future, what are some good things that you think will happen to you?

Unit 10
Word Games

This unit contains sentence completion and "missing word" story completion activities based on the Harry Potter themes.

Sentence Completion

When Harry thinks about the deaths of people he cared about, he feels...

When I think of the person who died, I feel...

When people talk with Harry about his parents, he does not like it when...

When people talk about the person who died, I don't like it when...

When Harry's aunt and uncle are not honest with him about the way Harry's parents died, he feels...

When people are not honest with me about the person who died or the person's death, I feel...

When Harry has questions or needs someone to listen to him, he...

When I have a question, I can ask...

Harry feels sad when he...

I feel sad when I...

When Harry feels sad, he gets support from...

When I feel sad, I can get support from...

In the wizarding world, when a person dies they...

When a person dies, I believe they...

Harry has several best friends who he can talk with about anything. My best friend is...

Some of the things I can talk with her/him about are...

Missing Word Stories

For these activities, the facilitator asks the children for different words to fill in the story. The facilitator should not read the story to the children until all the words are gathered.

The Surprise

A nice child named Scott was just waking up, when he looked out his window in his bedroom and saw _____ (**a magical creature**), and it was flying. "I think I will go outside and see what it is doing flying around my window." When he got outside, he noticed that the creature had a letter that it dropped right into Scott's hands. The letter was addressed to _____ (**the child's name**). "Wow," said Scott, "I'd better get this to _____ (**the child's name**) right away." Scott jumped on his _____ (**something you clean with, but not a broom**) and flew away. He couldn't ride his broom because it was in the shop getting fixed. Scott arrived at _____ (**child's name**)'s house and handed her/him the letter. The letter was from _____ (**the person who died**), and read _____ (**something the child would like to hear from the person who died**). "Thank you," said _____ (**the child's name**). "What a nice message. I will remember it always."

Discussion: What is a message the child would like to receive from the person who died? What message would the child write to the person who died? Who or what would deliver the message the child would write to the person who died?

A Wish Come True

A child, named _____ (**a name of a child**) was walking along the road near a castle one day and saw a beautiful _____ (**name of an object that you feel is pretty**). _____ (**the child's name**) picked up the _____ (**pretty object #1**) and looked at it for a long time. As she/he was looking at it, she/he realized that it had magical powers, and she/he could make a wish. She/he thought for a very long time and then she/he wished for _____ (**something you really want**). The wish came true! _____ (**the child's name**) was so happy that she/he _____ (**something someone does when she/he is happy**). She/he could hardly believe that her/his wish had come true. She/he was going to take the _____ (**pretty object #1**) with her/him, but realized that if she/he left it where she/he found it that maybe another child would find it and make a wish too. _____ (**the child's name**) set down the _____ (**pretty object #1**) on the ground by the _____ (**object you might find on a road**), and walked away.

Discussion: What is one wish you would make? If the wish came true, how would you feel? Who would you tell about the wish coming true? What might the person you would tell about your wish say to you? If the person who died heard about your wish, what might she or he say?

A Dream

One night a child named _____ (**a child's name**) had a dream that she/he was at the place people go after they die. As _____ (**the child's name**) entered this place she/he saw a beautiful _____ (**something you think is beautiful**) that was colored _____ (**your favorite color**). She/he just stood and looked at it for a long time. Suddenly _____ (**the person who died**) came up to her/him, hugged her/him and said _____ (**something someone might say to you after not seeing you for a long time**). _____ (**the child's name**) was thrilled to see (**the person who died**). As they talked, she/he told _____ (**the person who died**) how much she/he missed _____ (**something you miss about the person who died**). _____ (**the person who died**) said she/he missed that too. After they talked for awhile, _____ (**the person who died**) said that she/he needed to go, and that _____ (**the child's name**) needed to wake up. When _____ (**the child's name**) woke up she/he felt _____ (**an emotion that you like to feel**). She/he was glad that she/he had the dream.

Discussion: What do you think a place you may go after you die would look like? What colors might you see in this place? What might you say to the person who died when you met her/him in this place? What might the person who died say to you? What is one of the first things you and the person who died might do when you met in this place? Why would you do that activity?

My Favorite Memory

One day when I was in school, I thought about one of my favorite people named _____ (**the person who died**), who died. I felt _____ (**a happy emotion**) when I thought about _____ (**the person who died**), because of all the memories I have of her/him. I remember once when she/he _____ (**a favorite memory**). I also remember _____ (**another favorite memory**). It is sad that she/he has died. We can't do things together anymore. I miss all the things we use to do together. _____ (**the person who died**) use to say _____ (**something the person who died use to say**). When I remember what she/he said, I feel _____ (**an emotion that you like to feel**). I know that _____ (**the person who died**) will always be with me because she/he is in my heart and mind.

Discussion: What do you remember about the person who died? What is your favorite memory of the person who died? Do you believe that the person who died has memories? What memories might she/he have of times you and she/he spent together?

Unit 11
SOLACE THE STORY
DRAGON ACTIVITY

This activity can be used as a read-out-loud story for a younger child to finish, a coloring book for a child to finish, or a book for the child to illustrate and finish.

Basic Story

Solace the Story Dragon loved to read books to children. She would fly from library to library, and school to school, looking for children to read to. One day, as she was flying through the air, she saw a child sitting on a swing. Even though she was flying so high up in the clouds, she could still hear that the child was crying. She flew down and landed by the child. She asked them why they were crying. They told her that they were sad because someone they cared about had died. Solace wanted to help.

What comes next?

Coloring Book Version found on Worksheets 73-77

Cover:

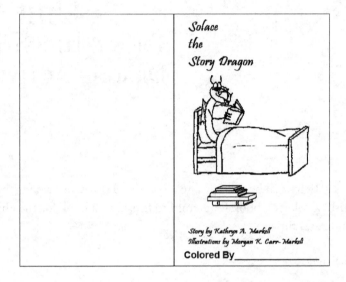

Solace the Story Dragon loved to read books to children.

She would fly from library to library, and school to school, looking for children to read to.

Even though she was flying so high up in the clouds, she could still hear that the child was crying.

One day, as she was flying through the air, she saw a child sitting on a swing.

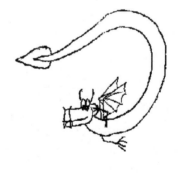

She flew down and landed by the child. She asked them why they were crying.

They told her that they were sad because someone they cared about had died. Solace wanted to help.

What Comes Next?

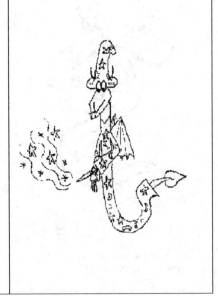

The children draw their own pictures version found on Worksheets 78-81.

Solace the Story Dragon loved
to read books to children.

She would fly from library to library, and
school to school, looking for children to
read to.

Even though she was flying so high up
in the clouds, she could still hear that
the child was crying.

One day, as she was flying through the
air, she saw a child sitting on a swing.

She flew down and landed by the child. She asked them why they were crying.

They told her that they were sad because someone they cared about had died. Solace wanted to help.

What comes next?

_____

_____

4

More Craft Ideas

The ideas presented in this section could be used with any of the book themes already presented or they could be used as stand-alone activities for grieving children and adolescents.

Unit 12
No-Sew Themed Scarves or Blankets

This project lets children or adolescents decorate fleece scarves or blankets with designs related to one of the books, and lets them attach a picture of the person they cared about inside the scarf, or on the inside of the blanket, so that it will be next to them.

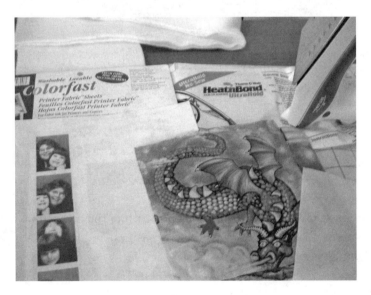

Materials needed:

- Enough fleece to make a scarf (⅓ to ½ yard depending on how wide you want it to be) or a blanket (2 to 2½ yards depending on how long you want it to be).
- A printer fabric sheet (There are many types available. The one shown here is Colorfast by June Tailor. It is available in three-sheet packs)
- ½ yard of an iron-on adhesive (I recommend HeatnBond UltraHold)
- About ½ yard of 100% cotton fabric depicting whatever theme you choose
- Photo or photos to scan into a computer

The directions that follow are for a scarf like the one shown above with fabric designs attached on the outer edges, and a photo attached to the middle inside of the scarf:

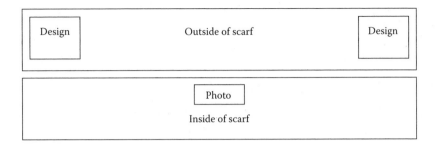

Directions:

1. Cut the fleece scarf to the desired width and length. There is no need to sew the edges of fleece.
2. Cut squares or other desired shapes from the fabric to be attached to the outside edges at each of the scarf ends.
3. Following the "HeatnBond' directions, iron the paper-backed adhesive onto each fabric piece.
4. Next, place the fleece scarf on an ironing board, and place the fabric pieces in the desired places on the outside ends of the scarf. **IMPORTANT: before ironing** the fabric pieces onto the scarf, **cover the scarf with a thin towel.** Ironing directly onto fleece **can melt** the fleece fabric.
5. **With a towel over the fabric and fleece,** iron the fabric pieces onto the fleece. They will now be attached to the fleece.
6. Following the printer sheet directions, scan your desired photo onto one of the photosheets.
7. Next, cut the photo out of the sheet, and follow the 'HeatnBond' directions again. Attach the paper-backed adhesive to the back of the fabric photo.
8. Now, place the photo in the desired position on the inside of the scarf, and **remembering to cover the fabric photo and fleece with a towel,** iron the photo to the fleece.

A fleece blanket could be made the same way, adhering fabric designs to the outside of the blanket, and fabric photos to the inside of the blanket.

Unit 13
OTHER NO-SEW FABRIC PROJECTS

The ideas outlined in Unit 12 for attaching fabric and fabric photos to fleece can be used to attach fabric and fabric photos to cloth bags, paper folders, paper book marks and other similar objects.

Decorate a Paper Folder with Fabric:

1. Choose a fabric (100% cotton works best) that fits with one of the book themes (even ¼ of a yard can decorate several folders).
2. Cut out a desired shape from the fabric, and following the HeatnBond directions, attach the adhesive to the fabric piece.
3. Place the fabric wherever desired on the paper folder. **Important: Place a towel over the folder and fabric piece before you iron the fabric onto the folder.**
4. Now, **with the towel over the fabric and folder,** iron the fabric onto the folder. It will now be attached.
5. Since the folder is paper, you could glue a paper photo of the person who has died to the inside or outside of the folder, if desired.

Decorate a Fabric Bag with Fabric:

1. Choose a fabric (100% cotton works best) that fits with one of the book themes
2. Cut out a desired shape from the fabric, and following the HeatnBond directions, attach the adhesive to the fabric piece.
3. Place the fabric wherever desired on the fabric or canvas bag. **Important: Place a towel over the fabric piece and bag before you iron the fabric onto the bag.**
4. Following the printer sheet directions, scan your desired photo onto one of the photosheets.
5. Next, cut the photo out of the sheet, and following the HeatnBond directions again, attach the paper-backed adhesive to the back of the fabric photo.
6. Now, place the photo in the desired position on the inside or outside of the bag, and **remembering to cover the fabric photo and bag with a towel,** iron the photo to the bag.

Unit 14
MAKING MEMORY BOXES

Children and adolescents may want to make "memory boxes" to honor and remember the person who died. These boxes could be kept as keepsakes, or they could be used as pencil boxes, etc., depending on what the child or adolescent desires. Having a pencil or even lunch box that has a picture of the person who died inside of it can make the child feel that they are bringing that person "with them" everyday. The picture could be in an inside cover or some other private place, if the child wants to keep the picture private.

Decorating Wood and Papier Mâché Boxes with Photos, Paint and Fabric:

Inexpensive wooden boxes and papier mâché boxes are available at many craft stores, and if purchased by the dozen, at www.orientaltradingcompany.com.

Suggestions for painting a box and attaching a photo to the bottom of the box:

1. Inexpensive acrylic paint works well on papier mâché and wood. There are many brands available; the one shown here is Crafters Edition Acrylic Paint. The child or adolescent could simply paint the boxes "free hand," taking time to allow sides to dry as the painting progresses. However, if the child would like to have more complicated designs, perhaps related to one of the book themes, they could trace stencils onto the box with pencil, and then paint the drawn designs. Inexpensive stencil books are available at http://store.doverpublications.com/by-subject-children-dover-little-activity-books-stencils.html. Stickers, beads, and other material could also be used to decorate the box.

2. Fabric could be attached to the boxes with glue. For example in the picture shown above, the top of the star box was traced onto a piece of fabric. That design could then be cut from the fabric and glued to the top of the

box. There are many glues available: I recommend Aleene's Original Tacky Glue.

3. A photo of the person who died could be photocopied or scanned into a computer, and the copy could be glued to the inside or outside of the box, as the child or adolescent desires.

Unit 15
DECORATING PICTURE FRAMES

Many inexpensive wooden frames are available from craft stores. Children and adolescents may want to make a frame for a special photograph of the person who died.

Suggestions for decorating wooden frames:

1. Inexpensive acrylic paints can be used to paint the frame. Again, as suggested in the Memory Box Activity, stencils, stickers, beads etc. could be used in the decoration process.
2. Pieces of fabric, perhaps related to a book theme or something that was important to the person who died, could be glued to the frame.
3. It is also possible to simply write words on the frame with permanent markers, as shown in the photo on page 171.

Unit 16
DECORATING PORCELAIN OBJECTS

Children or adolescents may like to decorate a plate or other porcelain object in memory of the person who died. In the photo above, an inexpensive "piggy-bank" (which could relate to the themes from the book *Charlotte's Web*) has been decorated with a word and design that is related to the book and also describes the person who died. The process used does not require any "firing," but the paints are permanent, and so children should not wear clothing that could be ruined etc. while using the paints. The paints used here are DecoColor Paint Markers.

These paints can also be used to decorate rocks. Children or adolescents could collect smooth rocks that they like, wash them, and then paint designs or words on them to honor and remember the person who died.

Harry Potter Glossary

Animagi: a witch or wizard who can turn into an animal.

Aurors: a witch or wizard who catches bad wizards.

Boggart: creatures who like dark enclosed spaces. They change their shape to whatever they think will frighten a person most.

Death Eater: a follower of Lord Voldemort. The Death Eaters were used in Voldemort's war against the British wizarding government, the Ministry of Magic, and against Dumbledore's anti-Death Eater group called the Order of the Phoenix.

Deluminator: referred to as the "Put-Outer" until Book 7. It is a device invented and used by Professor Dumbledore that can absorb and later return light from lamps and other sources of light; it looks much like a cigarette lighter.

Dementor: hooded figures who suck happiness out of people.

Elder Wand: also known as the "Deathstick" and the "Wand of Destiny." It is thought to be the most powerful wand that exists and is made of elder wood. When its true master uses it, she or he cannot be defeated in a fight.

Galleons: a form of wizarding currency.

Gryffindor: one of the four houses in Hogwarts. Gryffindor's symbol is a lion and its ghost is Nearly Headless Nick.

Hogwarts Express: the train to Hogwarts. The Hogwarts Express leaves London from platform 9¾.

Horcrux: is a holder in which a witch or wizard hides a part of her or his soul for the purpose of gaining immortality. When a part of a witch's or wizard's soul is stored in a horcrux, the witch or wizard becomes immortal as long as the horcrux remains whole. A horcrux is generally hidden away in a safe location, and can be made from any object, even living matter.

Hufflepuff: one of the four houses in Hogwarts. Its symbol is a badger and its ghost is the Fat Friar.

Legilimency: the magical skill of removing feelings and memories from another person's mind — a sort of magical "mind-reading."

Muggle: non-magic people.

Nagini: a snake that was made into a horcrux by Voldemort. Because Voldemort did not know that he had unintentionally made Harry into a horcrux, Voldemort thought that Nagini was the final horcrux needed to split his soul into seven pieces.

Occlumency: the counter-skill to Legilimency. A witch or wizard can prevent a legilimens from discovering thoughts or memories which contradict one's spoken words, actions, or emotions.

Parseltongue: the language of snakes. Some witches and wizards can speak and understand it.

Patronus: A spell that can ward off Dementors; every wizard's Patronus has a different shape.

Pensieve: is a stone receptacle used for storing memories. A witch or wizard can take out memories and store them in the Pensieve to experience them later.

Portkey: can be set to transport anybody who touches it to a designated location.

Quidditch: a wizard sport that is played world-wide. It is played on broomsticks.

Seeker: attempts to catch the Golden Snitch before the other team's Seeker catches it.

Chasers: have to throw the Quaffle, a large ball, through one of the hoops to score a goal, getting ten points for every goal.

Keepers: one Keeper per team, whose job it is to stop the chasers from scoring.

Bludgers: two balls which can knock players off their brooms.

Beaters: two on each team, trying to knock the Bludgers toward the members from the other team.

Golden Snitch: a winged ball that when a Seeker catches it ends the game, getting an extra hundred and fifty points.

Ravenclaw: one of the four houses in Hogwarts. Its symbol is an eagle and its ghost is the Gray Lady.

Remembrall: a ball that lights up when you forget something that you need to do.

Resurrection Stone: is used to see and communicate with people who have died.

Riddikulus: a spell that will stop the Boggarts from showing what is fearful and turns the fearful image into something funny or ridiculous.

Slytherin: one of the four houses in Hogwarts. Its symbol is a serpent and its ghost is the Bloody Baron.

St. Mungo's Hospital for Magical Maladies and Injuries: (generally referred to just as St. Mungo's Hospital) the wizarding hospital of Britain.

Thestral: a creature that has a horse-like appearance that only people who have witnessed death can see.

Transfiguration: the transforming of something into something else.

Triwizard Tournament: a competition between the three major wizard schools in Britain: Hogwarts, Beauxbatons and Durmstrang. One person from each of these schools competes in magical contests for a prize of 1,000 Galleons.

Triwizard Cup: the trophy for the one who wins the Triwizard Tournament.

Whomping Willow: a tree that will hit anyone or anything that comes near it.

Adapted from:

http://www.harrypotterfanclub.com/dictionary.htm
http://www.tikah.co.il/english/harry/extras/dictionary/dictionary.html
http://en.wikipedia.org
http://www.harrypotterfacts.com/index.htm

These are not official Harry Potter sites.

References

Alcott, Louisa May (1868). *Little Women*. Boston: Roberts Brothers. Retrieved August 26, 2007 from http://ia331312.us.archive.org/3/items/littlewomenormeg00alcoiala/littlewomenormeg00alcoiala.pdf .

Burnett, F. B. (1911). *The Secret Garden*. New York: HarperCollins Publishers.

Doka, K. (2002). *Disenfranchised Grief*. Illinois: Research Press.

Greig, Geordie (2006). There Would Be So Much To Tell Her..., *The Daily Telegraph*. Retrieved January 15, 2007 from http://www.telegraph.co.uk/news/main.jhtml?xml=/news/2006/01/10/nrowl110.xml.

Gibbs, N. (2003). The Real Magic of Harry Potter, *Time Magazine*. Retrieved January 15, 2007 from http://www.time.com/time/magazine/article/0,9171,1101030623-458732,00.html.

Guest, J. (1976). *Ordinary People*. New York: Viking Press.

Haber, D. (2005). Dumbledore Is Not Dead. Retrieved June 30, 2005 from http://www.beyondhogwarts.com/harry-potter/topics/dumbledoreisnotdead.html.

Lawless, J. (2007). Harry's Story Comes to a Definite End, *The Seattle Times*. Retrieved September 1, 2007 from http://seattletimes.nwsource.com/html/entertainment/2003796881_webrowling19.html.

Meltz, B. (2005). Young Potter Readers Need to Talk, Grieve, *The Boston Globe*. Retrieved July 30, 2005 from http://www.boston.com/ae/books/articles/2005/07/21/young_potter_readers_need_to_talk_grieve.

Readers Respond to New Harry Potter Book (2005). CBS4Denver. Retrieved January 10, 2007 from http://cbs4denver.com/entertainment/Harry.Potter.J.2.255699.html.

Rogers, Dale Evans (2004). Angel Unaware, *50th Anniversary Edition*. Tarrytown, NY: Fleming H. Revell Company.

Rawls, W. (1961). *Where the Red Fern Grows*. New York: Doubleday.

Rowling, J. K. (1997). *Harry Potter and the Sorcerer's Stone*. New York: Arthur A. Levine Books.

Rowling, J. K. (1999). *Harry Potter and the Chamber of Secrets*. New York: Arthur A. Levine Books.

Rowling, J. K. (1999). *Harry Potter and the Prisoner of Azkaban*. New York: Arthur A. Levine Books.

Rowling, J. K. (2000). *Harry Potter and the Goblet of Fire*. New York: Arthur A. Levine Books.

Rowling, J. K. (2003). *Harry Potter and the Order of the Phoenix*. New York: Arthur A. Levine Books.

Rowling, J. K. (2005). *Harry Potter and the Half-Blood Prince*. New York: Arthur A. Levine Books.

Rowling, J. K. (2007). *Harry Potter and the Deathly Hallows*. New York: Arthur A. Levine Books.

Seligman, M.E.P. (1995). *The Optimistic Child*. New York: Houghton Mifflin.

Sidney, Margaret (1881). *Five Little Peppers and How They Grew*. Lothrop, Lee & Shepard. Retrieved August 26, 2007 from http://manybooks.net/titles/sidneymaetext015lpep10.html.

Vieira, M. (2007). Harry Potter: The Final Chapter Interview with J. K. Rowling, Dateline, NBC. Retrieved August 2, 2007 from http://www.msnbc.msn.com/id/20001720/.

White, E. B. (1952). *Charlotte's Web*. New York: HarperCollins.

Index